# Leaders Assemble! Leadership in the MCU

# EXPLORING EFFECTIVE LEADERSHIP PRACTICES THROUGH POPULAR CULTURE

**Series editor:** Michael Urick

The aim of this series is to examine modern and innovative business theories and methods via relatable popular cultural themes. The books will provide academically rigorous and credible applications and solutions to practitioners and upper level business students, in a format designed to be highly engaging and effective.

Titles in Exploring Effective Leadership Practices through Popular Culture:

A Manager's Guide to Using the Force: Leadership Lessons from a Galaxy Far Far Away
*Michael Urick*

Leadership in Middle Earth: Theories and applications for organizations
*Michael Urick*

You Win or You Die: Leadership Lessons from Kings and Queens
*Nathan Tong and Michael Urick*

Cross-Cultural Leadership in the Four Nations: Lessons from Avatar The Last Airbender
*Sy Islam and Gordon Schmidt*

Leadership Insights for Wizards and Witches
*Aditya Simha*

# Leaders Assemble! Leadership in the MCU

BY

**GORDON B. SCHMIDT**
*University of Louisiana- Monroe, USA*

AND

**SY ISLAM**
*Farmingdale State College, USA*

United Kingdom – North America – Japan – India – Malaysia – China

Emerald Publishing Limited
Howard House, Wagon Lane, Bingley BD16 1WA, UK

First edition 2022

**Reprints and permissions service**
Contact: permissions@emeraldinsight.com

**British Library Cataloguing in Publication Data**
A catalogue record for this book is available from the British Library

ISBN: 978-1-80117-673-6 (Print)
ISBN: 978-1-80117-670-5 (Online)
ISBN: 978-1-80117-672-9 (Epub)

ISOQAR certified
Management System,
awarded to Emerald
for adherence to
Environmental
standard
ISO 14001:2004.

ISOQAR
REGISTERED
Certificate Number 1985
ISO 14001

INVESTOR IN PEOPLE

*Gordon dedicates this book to his wife, his sister-in-law who had to watch superhero movies she never wanted to see, and his family of Schmidts, Wiegands, Smiths, and Hartmans. He also specifically dedicates this book to his father, who in buying a box of comic books at the Fireman's Flea Market exposed him to his first Marvel hero comic favorites, Spiderman and the Avengers.*

*Sy dedicates this book to his family: his brother, Sohel, who gave Sy his first comics and a never-ending love of the medium; to his parents Amin and Naziba who kept buying him comics even though they didn't want to; and to his wife, Rownak, who is his forever MCU movie date.*

*We both also dedicate this book to all the writers, artists, creators, and actors who brought us the amazing Marvel Universe in its comic and movie forms.*

# Contents

# About the Authors

**Gordon B. Schmidt**, PhD, is a Professor of Management at the University of Louisiana Monroe. He has a doctorate in Organizational Psychology from Michigan State University. He researches the Future of Work and how technology is changing the nature of company–employee relations today, which has been published in a number of academic journals. He co-edited a book with Richard Landers on how social media is used in selection and recruitment. He does research related to virtual leadership and how technology impacts the leadership process. He has done research related to the gig economy and the communities of gig workers who have sprung up around crowdsourcing sites like Amazon Mechanical Turk. He has written about the future of the field of I-O Psychology related to outreach of the field to those in practice. He also researches leadership and/or motivation in varied contexts including lean production, corporate social responsibility initiatives, job apathy, and popular culture.

He teaches courses in organizational behavior, training methods, employee relations, organizational development, organizational theory, leadership, and human resources. His work related to teaching has been presented at conferences and published in a number of journals. He won a teaching excellence award from his college in 2015. He acted as the program chair for the 2020 virtual Management and Organizational Behavior Teaching Society Conference. He is the incoming co-editor for the journal *Management Teaching Review*.

He consults with organizations, primarily related to leadership, motivation, and social media-related areas.

**Sy Islam**, PhD, has over 10 years of experience in a variety of corporate, academic, and applied settings. He is an Associate Professor of Industrial Organizational Psychology at Farmingdale State College where he teaches courses related to training and leadership development. He has conducted research on team adaptation, social media in hiring, and consumer feedback via social media. In addition to his role as a professor, he is a co-founder and vice president of Consulting with Talent Metrics. In his role at Talent Metrics, he develops solutions for organizations in training and development, selection, survey design, performance management, and team building. He has served as the president of the Long Island Chapter of the Association for Talent Development and co-chair of the People Analytics Special Interest Group at ATD NYC. He is the winner of the SIOP Presidential Recognition Award and a Faculty Mentorship award from Farmingdale State College's Center for Teaching, Learning and Technology.

# Acknowledgments

Many people helped with the creation of this book and its inspiration. We would first of all like to thank our families for their love and support during this book writing process.

We would like to thank Michael Urick for developing the great idea of the "Exploring Effective Leadership Practices through Popular Culture" series. When we heard of this series, it felt like something we wanted to read and contribute to. Mike has given us great support as the series editor and been generous in sharing examples and feedback. He has been a great person to work with and we are lucky to have his help.

We want to thank Fiona Allison at Emerald for all her support of our proposal and this book. Her support has been invaluable.

We also want to thank Aiswarya Mahathma Suritha for her work as our book project editor in making sure we got everything we needed in order and ready.

We want to thank all the researchers we cite within this book. Their important leadership research helps leaders to get better, and we hope this book will help spread their knowledge to new readers and leaders. We also want to thank Travis Langley for all his good work at connecting psychology to superheroes across his many books.

We also want to thank all the people who build that Marvel comic universe. We both grew up reading these comics and enjoy them to this day.

We also want to thank everyone who has worked on Marvel movies (even the less good ones) and the creators of the MCU who made a connected universe well in the spirit of the comics.

And thank you to you, the reader, for joining us on this leadership and MCU journey!

Chapter 1

# How We See Leadership in the Marvel Cinematic Universe and How We See Leadership in General

## Welcome to This Book

Today, superheroes' movies are perhaps the most popular genre of films, worldwide. The Marvel Cinematic Universe (MCU) films are the top grossing film franchise of all time (Whitten, 2021), and that number doesn't even include the large number of movies based on Marvel properties that have been released by other studios as well. These Marvel heroes are found across our media landscape, including streaming sites, video games, merchandise, and of course comics! Marvel heroes are ubiquitous in our lives.

This dominance of Marvel properties suggests that heroes and the ideas they represent resonate worldwide. Many of us grew up wanting to be superheroes or at least have a similar positive impact on the world.

While most of us will never engage in fights with supervillains, we all do have a chance to have a positive impact on those around us. One major way of doing so is through leadership, influencing other people and helping them to accomplish important things. By working together, we can accomplish more than what we could accomplish individually, as we see with superhero teams like the Avengers, X-men, and Guardians of the Galaxy.

While we may not be doing the same tasks as our favorite superheroes, there are many examples and lessons we can draw from Marvel films on how to become better leaders. This book is part of the series Exploring Effective Leadership Practices Through Popular Culture, which looks to help readers grow as leaders through lessons learned from popular culture. When we first heard about the series we were so excited and knew that we wanted to write about how the MCU can teach us about leadership.

This book will draw on leadership lessons and examples from the films, paired with academic research findings, to help you become a better leader. In this first chapter, we briefly introduce the films, why we think they are relevant to leadership, discuss how we see leadership, give an overview of our chapters, and help you to consider how best to use this book.

Leaders Assemble! Leadership in the MCU, 1–7

Copyright © 2022 by Gordon B. Schmidt and Sy Islam

Published under exclusive license by Emerald Publishing Limited

doi:10.1108/978-1-80117-670-520221001

## The Marvelous World of Marvel Movies and Comics

We think the MCU is particularly relevant for learning about leadership for a few major reasons. The first is that this film franchise is a shared universe of many characters. Characters like Iron Man and Captain America are protagonists of their own films but also come together in other films as members of teams. As protagonists and main characters of their own films, many Marvel characteristics have their own strong personalities and perspectives. So Marvel is made up of heroes with different ideas and perspectives interacting, coming into conflict, and ultimately saving the day. This is a messy world where everyone doesn't agree or get along, which makes it a good fit with how things happen in our real world. Our real world isn't made up of people who all see things the same way and just follow whatever a leader says to do. While the nature of conflict might look different in MCU movies, in our real lives, we all need to work together with people different from us and figure out how we can best work together to accomplish important tasks.

And these different perspectives can actually be a strength, as together we come up with ideas and solutions we wouldn't have on our own. Every Marvel movie is not just one person's vision but a wide range of people working together to make an engaging and enjoyable film. We need the director, actors, writers, special effects artists, and technicians to all work together to make a film happen. Their different skills and perspectives make the movie magic we get to all enjoy.

The comic books these films are based on were also created in this collaborative way, bringing in different perspectives from creators. When many of the major Marvel superheroes were created in the 1960s, Marvel used a unique method for creating the book which ended up being known as the Marvel Method (Daniels, 1991). In the Marvel Method, the writer of a comic comes up first with a relatively brief outline for what will be in the particular comic issue. This will often be the big plot elements of where the story starts and ends but usually doesn't spell out particular lines of dialogue or highly specific visual elements. This brief outline of the story is then given to the artist, who draws a full story out of it (Daniels, 1991). The artist has a major impact on how the story looks but also how the plot proceeds from start to end. What the artist adds can be a major part of the story, with some additions being as significant as characters being added (The hero the Silver Surfer came about due to an addition to the plot outline by artist Jack Kirby! Oakes, 2020). The fully drawn issue is then sent back to the writer who creates dialogue and narration based on what the artist has drawn. The book with dialogue is then passed on to an inker, who helps emphasize or de-emphasize parts of the art, and a letterer does the same for the dialogue. Thus, a Marvel Method comic is truly a deep collaboration between multiple parties to create an engaging story.

The writer and artist work together and bring their different sensibilities to make the story work, with the inker, letterer, and editor bringing their own perspectives and talents. Thus, the MCU is not just the creation of one writer like Stan Lee, Roy Thomas, Chris Claremont, Christopher Priest, or Brian Bendis but a true partnership as well with artists like Jack Kirby, Steve Ditko, and John

Romita Jr. The MCU films are a testament to creators working together to generate a strong story. As Kevin Feige, the producer and major mastermind of the MCU states "it really is a village to make this film, but they did let me lead" (Aurthur, 2021). A good story requires people working together, influencing each other to shape the story and make it successful. As you will see in the next section on how we see leadership, this influence and collaboration is something that is essential in leadership.

## How We See Leadership

Since this is a book about leadership and how you can become a better leader, it is important for you to understand our perspectives, as the authors, on what leadership is. Our definition of leadership draws on the work of Yukl and Gardner (2020) and Katz and Kahn (1978), as we see leadership as a process of influence where a leader influences another person to take action or think in a way that person would not have done so on their own. So leadership is about influencing people, changing their minds, and changing what actions they will take. This means leadership can have a big impact on the world, as things are happening because of that leader's influence that would not have happened on their own. And leadership is a process that we can get better at! You can become a better leader through experience, reflection, and through learning through books such as this and other works on leadership (Whetten & Cameron, 2020).

It is important to note that we are focusing on leadership as a process, not on a single designated "leader." When people talk about leaders too often they focus on CEOs or presidents or generals. Leadership is not reserved exclusively for those with fancy titles, all of us can (and do!) engage in leadership. We all influence coworkers or fellow students, friends, family, and others we meet. So while what you learn in this book will help you if you happen to be a CEO, it will still be helpful in any role you have in an organization and in your own daily life.

With our focus on people influencing each other, even without a formal leadership role, the perspective of this book also draws on the ideas of shared leadership. Shared leadership is the idea that there can be an interactive influence process in groups, where members of the group influence each other to help reach group goals (Pearce & Conger, 2003). So rather than one person who always is the leader or "boss," multiple people lead the group at times, often due to their particular expertise or skill set. We certainly believe in the real world it is rare that a designated leader is doing all of the influencing, rather team members are often influencing each other to help reach the team goal. A good leader may engage in leadership often but will many times be influenced by their followers in what to do. Leadership should go in both directions.

The MCU films show both these concepts. While a team like the Avengers might have somewhat of a boss like Nick Fury (for some of the films) and have people commonly engaging in leadership when the team is on a mission (Captain America and Iron Man), each Avenger has a skill set and expertise that lets them influence the team when it is relevant. For example, if the Avengers are fighting someone from Asgard, like Loki, Thor is often the one with the most knowledge in the situation and thus can influence what the group does. If the group is dealing with a tough science-related topic, Bruce Banner will often be looked to for guidance. If a covert operation is needed, the Black Widow will probably lead the discussion, not Thor. Each member leads at times and influences the others based on personal expertise.

Both authors of this book are also Industrial-Organizational Psychologists, so we bring that perspective to all that we do. Industrial-Organizational (I-O) Psychology is a field that applies psychological principles to organizations (Conte & Landy, 2019). We help to make organizational members both more effective in their jobs and more satisfied with what they do. We'll be drawing on relevant theories and research of I-O Psychology in this book, as well work in a whole range of relevant fields like management, leadership, industrial relations, and organizational behavior. Drawing on research will let us give you advice that is supported by evidence, rather than merely our opinions. This will help you to grow as a leader and successful employee. We all can grow and get better in what we do and hope this book helps your own growth.

## Organization of This Book

We have organized this book in the way we think generally best helps people to engage in the leadership concepts and examples for their own learning and reflection. However, you are welcome to read this book in whatever way makes the most sense to you. This section will highlight at a general level what each chapter is about. Each chapter focuses on a core leadership concept or two, with generally one MCU or Marvel film focused on. So you learn about the leadership concept through the academic research on the topic and the examples of it found within an MCU film. Table in the Appendix is a handy reference that includes each chapter title, the core leadership concepts, and which films are the foci of discussion.

Our first chapter (you are here!) welcomes readers to this book and discusses how this book is organized. It briefly introduces the MCU films and why we think they are helpful for learning about leadership. We also discuss how the authors see leadership, as a process and shared.

Our second chapter looks at leader transitions, succession planning, and the sources of leaders influence, through looking at Wakanda and Asgard. We then discuss how you might navigate such issues in your own organization.

Our third chapter looks at the ideas of shared leadership and how leaders can emerge using "Guardians of the Galaxy" to illustrate these concepts. We discuss how you might recognize opportunities for shared leadership and leadership emergence in your own contexts.

Our fourth chapter looks at how valuable peer and leader mentorship can be and how shared vision and perspective helps these processes through examples from "Spider-man into the Spider-verse" and other Spider-man films. The potential value of shared vision in mentorship in your own context is discussed.

Our fifth chapter looks at that nature of conflict, how conflict can be good in some circumstances, and the nature of negotiating a decision. "Captain

America: Civil War" and the Avengers films provide examples we can learn from. We then have you reflect on how you can handle conflicts more successfully when you engage in leadership.

Our sixth chapter considers how stress and crisis impact our mental state and our ability to engage in effective leadership through examples found in "Avengers Infinity War" and other films. While we hope none of us have to deal with stress the level of Thanos, we help you draw lessons of pitfalls of the leadership process during stress and how you can best lead in challenging times.

Our seventh chapter looks at how being authentic can help people to be a better leader, but it often requires significant self-awareness, reflection, and personal growth. We follow the path of Tony Star across the Iron Man and Avenger films to show this struggle we can experience as a leader, even with good intentions. We have you reflect on your own authenticity and self-awareness as a leader and how you can grow in both.

Our eighth chapter discusses the important roles leaders play in external relationships with those outside the group, with "Black Panther" and the example of potentially revealing the true Wakanda to the world. You are asked to consider how your own leadership roles involve such external relationships and how those relationships should be managed.

Our ninth chapter highlights how important leaders are in helping followers make sense of their connection with and identity related to an organization. We do this by looking across X-men films and how different leaders define mutants as heroes, X-men, mutants, or even menaces. We discuss how you can impact how others see their place in an organization and the world at large.

Our 10th chapter looks at the importance of female leadership and how women can be relegated to supporting roles in both the MCU and in the real world due to implicit theories of what a leader should look or act like. We caution you to not relegate potentially great female leaders to supporting roles and how you can combat these implicit leadership biases in real-life organizations.

Our 11th chapter focuses on the idea of servant leadership, illustrated in the MCU by Captain America. We talk about how Steve Rogers can be an inspiration and example for you in your own leadership actions and willingness to take ethical stands.

Our 12th chapter focuses on how leaders form teams based on their own goals. Nick Fury, Professor X, and Magneto are looked at as examples of how leaders can go about recruiting and selecting members for their team. You are advised to consider how you should select team members based on your team goals.

Our 13th and last chapter draws ideas and takeaways from across the other chapters to summarize major actions you can take to become a more effective leader in your own life. You should leave this chapter with a clear idea of what to do next to become a better leader.

## How to Use This Book

While our general recommendation is for you to read this book straight through, depending on your own experiences and situation it may make sense to do otherwise. Here we outline some general recommendations based on your own experiences and role.

The first distinction is how big of a Marvel movie fan you are. If you are a big fan of the MCU films, you may know these movies by heart. For someone like you, you know what happens in the films, but this book helps you see things in a new, leadership-focused light. We would expect that as we talk about leadership concepts, you will start to think about many other examples of a concept within the films. For a big Marvel movie fan, it probably makes sense to read this book in the order of this book as written, but feel free to jump ahead to your favorites as desired. The table in the Appendix can help you to see where particular films are mentioned.

If you are a more casual fan, you may not remember film events as well and may in fact have not seen some of the films we discuss. That is perfectly ok, too! Each chapter will summarize major aspects of the film so you can follow along. The table in the Appendix will help you to know which films are being talked about in which chapters. For the casual fan, there are two ways you can interact with the films and this book. You could read the book chapter first to learn the concepts and then watch the relevant film to see the concepts in action. You could also do the reverse, watch the film and then read the chapter, so when you see the examples mentioned in the chapter, they will be fresh in your mind. Either is a reasonable choice, so you might want to try both ways and see which best helps your learning from this book.

The second distinction is your current relationship with leadership. If you are someone currently in a leadership position (or teaching about leadership), draw on your own experiences as we discuss leadership concepts. You will want to think about how the leadership concepts and examples apply in your own leadership situation. You may also consider how concepts from this book might be worth communicating to your followers, other leaders, or your students/trainees. If you have a current leadership issue (or are teaching a certain topic), feel free to skip ahead to a chapter that seems like it will be helpful.

If you are an aspiring leader or current student, you may not be in a current leadership role, but as we have mentioned before all of us engage in leadership in our everyday lives. So if you consider your own life experiences, you might find you have more leadership experiences than you thought. You may also want to think about leaders you've interacted with in your life and the type of leader you want to be someday. For people in this group, it makes sense to read this book through in the given order, although if you are a student make sure to read this book in the way your instructor tells you!

## Summary

In this chapter, we introduced the big picture of this book. We talked about the MCU and how important collaboration was to both the films and the comics source material.

We then discussed how we see leadership and why leadership is important. Leadership is a process of influence and we all engage in leadership in our lives.

Leadership is often shared, with different people acting as the leader in different situations. The MCU and other Marvel films offer many great examples of leadership that we can learn from.

We then talked about the organization of this book overall and gave brief summaries of what to expect in each book chapter.

Finally, we talked about different ways this book could be used depending on your knowledge of the MCU and relationship to leadership.

We want to thank you for picking up this book. As two lifelong Marvel fans, it is a real dream come true to have written this. We hope this book helps your own leadership journey and you enjoy it. Leaders Assemble!

Chapter 2

# Who Has a Right to Be the Leader?
# Leadership Transitions in Black Panther

Throughout the films *Captain America: Civil War and Black Panther*, we see a discussion of who can be considered for leadership roles. Decisions around who will be selected as a leader are often referred to as succession planning for leadership transitions (Froelich, McKee, & Rathge, 2011). Leadership transitions are exceptionally important for organizations. In Civil War, T'Challa is shocked by the assassination of his father, T'Chaka which throws the leadership of Wakanda into question. In Black Panther, T'Challa is challenged by other potential candidates for the throne of Wakanda like M'Baku and Erik Killmonger.

Leadership transitions are important to organizations to maintain continuity and flow. In this chapter, we will discuss how we can recruit potential leaders, select the best leaders, and how concepts such as legitimacy and the bases of power impact potential leaders. Finally, we'll discuss how you can use this information to identify potential leaders in your organization and help them transition into leadership roles.

## Who is a Potential Leader?

Before we can select a leader, we need to determine who can potentially be a leader within an organization. Recruiting and selecting the right leaders for an organization is a challenge faced by many organizations. The examples of leadership transitions in the Marvel Cinematic Universe (MCU) contain a common thread: they are often transitions between royalty. When King T'Chaka is assassinated in Civil War, the implicit assumption is that T'Challa, his son and heir, will become the next Black Panther and the leader of Wakanda. A similar pattern is found in the Thor series, where Odin has already designated that Thor will be his heir as long as he's deemed worthy. The question of who is worthy and why is important to leadership decisions. How do organizations without a royal bloodline recruit and select effective leaders?

Leadership recruitment is a challenge even during the best of economic times because successful leaders tend to be employed and their employers plan on keeping them in their positions. Since organizations often don't have a king and queen

Leaders Assemble! Leadership in the MCU, 9–15
Copyright © 2022 by Gordon B. Schmidt and Sy Islam
Published under exclusive license by Emerald Publishing Limited
doi:10.1108/978-1-80117-670-520221002

giving birth to their next leader they must recruit new leaders through peer referrals, social media networking, and professional societies (McEntire & Green-
Shortridge, 2011). An organization needs to find an appropriate leader and these
sources can often help to identify high-potential leadership talent. Peer referrals
are very useful to identify potential leaders who are a good fit for the organization
(Kaul, 2021). Professional societies can also provide useful candidates for consideration for leadership positions. Social media has provided a cutting-edge new
tool to help organizations recruit new potential leader. Social media expands the
reach of an organization to find leadership candidates outside of the traditional
sources used by an organization (McFarland & Ployhart, 2015). Ultimately, your
goal as an organization is to find a leader who can guide your organization into
the future.

In addition to their blood ties to previous kings both T'Challa and Thor must
prove their worth. T'Challa must prove his worth by hunting down his father's
assassin. Back in Wakanda, T'Challa must also face challengers from the various
tribes to prove that he has the strength to lead Wakanda as the Black Panther.
Thor is initially sent to Earth by Odin for leading an unsanctioned attack on
the Frost Giants. Odin makes it clear that Thor will not return to Asgard and
reclaim his position as heir unless he learns to be worthy of the power of Mjolnir,
the mystic hammer. When your organization considers leadership job applicants
whether internally or externally, assessments must be made of the qualifications
of the applicants. McEntire and Green-Shortridge (2011) suggests the use of
behavioral and psychological assessments to determine if an applicant has the
necessary qualities to be a leader. Not every organization has a waterfall ready
for a one-on-one duel between candidates, thus pre-hire assessments must suffice.
Personality inventories that measure a leader's personality have been found to be
an effective tool in predicting leader behavior (Hogan, Curphy, & Hogan, 1994).
The goal of these tools is to help organizations make better decisions about who
should be considered for leadership roles. Ideally, these tools would be as objective as possible and would allow for a diverse potential pool of leadership talent
to enter the leadership development pipeline.

Unlike traditional royal lines where leadership is passed from parent to
child, organizations must build leadership pipelines. Your organization can
start to determine who might be a good leader by identifying key leadership
competencies. In other words, what makes a good leader in your organization?
Even in the MCU, the leader of Asgard may not be a good leader in Wakanda.
Employees who show important leadership skills within your organization's
competency model should be selected into your leadership development program.
Those employees who have been deemed high potentials are often selected into
leadership development pipelines (Groves, 2007). In the same way that Thor or
T'Challa would receive specialized education and training to prepare them for
leadership, high-potential leadership candidates are also placed into specialized
learning programs. Fulmer, Stumpf, and Bleak (2009) found that in order for
organizations to maintain a strong pipeline of leaders, they needed to identify
talent using objective assessments (i.e., personality inventories, tests), specialized
learning programs (i.e., leadership training), and rotational programs. T'Challa

and Thor both received special knowledge and experiences traveling and learning outside their respective worlds to gain necessary skills to be king. In organizations, leadership development programs may take the form of formal coursework, mentorship programs, or rotation programs for high-potential leadership candidates. These programs are built to support the organization by developing leadership competencies in high-potential candidates.

One challenge in identifying high-potential talent for organizations that you should be aware of when developing a high-potential leadership program is gender and racial bias. The examples cited in this chapter are men from royal lineages, indicating a high socioeconomic status (SES). But leadership talent can be found across the spectrum of age, gender, ethnicity, and SES. Greer and Virick (2008) highlight the importance of using objective talent assessments to identify high-potential leaders from within the workforce. In addition to objective assessment, a clear succession process is key to identifying future leaders. These concerns are not found in the MCU where succession through patrilineal monarchy (i.e., Asgard) eschews the need for diverse leadership.

In Wakanda, because of the patrilineal system of royal heritage, talented individuals like Naka, Ramonda, and Okoye are not considered for the top position of Black Panther until the most dire of circumstances. Despite all of them serving in important leadership roles within Wakanda, they are not readily considered for the highest position. This is a loss for Wakanda as much as it is for them individually. This situation extends to Asgard where talented Asgardians like Sif are not considered for leadership roles. Organizations with more effective leadership pipelines would not miss out on talented individuals who could serve as potentially effective leaders.

## Making the Case for Leadership

A question of leadership for both T'Challa and Thor is the question of worth. Who is worthy to lead these ancient kingdoms? Both men are considered potential leaders for their kingdoms, but the question of whether they are worthy to serve as a leader is an important one. In the previous section, we discussed ways by which you could assess leadership potential. However, many people in their respective organizations need to be able to show worth in other ways beyond objective assessments. In organizations, the question of worth is one of qualifications or of power. The type of power an individual exerts has an impact on their leadership role within an organization and the perception of that role's legitimacy.

Within organizations, people derive power from a variety of different sources. Researchers formalized these bases of power into a taxonomy that allows leaders and followers to know where they may derive power. Broadly these bases of power can be categorized into two areas: (a) position power and (b) personal power. Position power is power rooted in an individual's role. For example, the one with the mantle of Black Panther commands the armies of Wakanda. That is embedded into the position. Personal power has to do with the relationships that the individual has that make them a leader (French & Raven, 1962).

The first base of power is referent power which is based on how much followers like the leader. When T'Challa is preparing for the waterfall ceremony, his sister Shuri makes it seem as though T'Challa's coronation is inevitable because everyone knows that he is the true king. This is an example of referent power. During this moment on the waterfall there is a sense of palpable joy at the prospect of T'Challa taking on the mantle of Black Panther. T'Challa is adored not only by his family but by the other tribes and that is one source of his power and provides legitimacy to his potential reign as the new king. One way that individuals within organizations can start to build a case for themselves as a leader is by building their relationships with others. If you want people to follow you, they often have to at least like you.

Some leaders have power based on their expertise. Shuri has expertise and can exert her leadership within the royal family because of her scientific knowledge. She can advise her brother on matters of science including improving his costume, providing weapons and additional support during missions. Despite her age, her expertise makes her a valuable member of the royal family. Many people may feel hesitant to take on leadership roles but if you can stress your knowledge in a particular area and describe what you are capable of, your colleagues may begin to treat you like a leader. The first step in achieving leadership is having your skills recognized, some of that comes from being an expert.

Similar to expert power is power based on information. Information power is based on what an individual knows about a particular situation. Much of informational power comes from the role that an individual plays. For example, the priest Zuri has informational power. He knows the secrets of the herb that provides the Black Panther with his superhuman strength. Zuri knows how to give that power and how to take that power away. In your organization, you can reflect on who has information power. In some cases, it's the employees who determine your level of access to computer files and information within your organization. They control what you have access to and thus what information you have about the organization.

Another base of power in French and Raven's model is reward power. Reward power is defined as a leader's ability to provide rewards to others. An interesting display of reward power can be seen in the interaction between T'Challa and Agent Ross. At the time Agent Ross believes that Wakanda is a backward nation and believes that Wakanda should freely accept the help of the US government. Ross tries to exert this power over T'Challa during their interaction. T'Challa also shows his ability to provide rewards when he meets with his friend W'Kabi. W'Kabi has a long-standing grievance against the villain Klaw, who murdered W'Kabi's parents. T'Challa promises to bring Klaw back to Wakanda to bring justice to him. W'Kabi deeply desires this reward because he wants revenge. The failure to deliver on this reward harms T'Challa later when Killmonger delivers Klaw's body to W'Kabi upon entry to Wakanda.

Think about your own experiences in the workplace. How does reward power impact who you view as a leader? Rewards are potent motivational tools that leaders can use in a variety of ways. Some rewards are formal and are embedded in your role at work. Others are more contextual and based around items of value that others may desire. For example, if you control scheduling in your workplace that is a form of reward power. Traditional forms of reward power include the ability to assign bonuses, approve vacation days, and certify increases in salary.

Oftentimes, reward power is associated with another form of power called legitimate power. Legitimate power is a formal type of power that is derived from an individual's position within an organization. In Black Panther, General Okoye has legitimate power over the Dora Milaje. When she gives a command, it is based on her role as general and as the acknowledged leader of Dora Milaje. If you want to know what you have legitimate power over, the easiest place to start is your job description and the organizational chart. Consider your direct supervisor. The organization has designated your supervisor as having some control over your work. This is the surest form of legitimate power. In Black Panther, the battle between Killmonger and T'Challa is a question of legitimate power. Who is the true heir? The other forms of power are used to try to achieve the legitimacy found in the role of Black Panther. We see this legitimacy during the final battle, when the armies of Wakanda respond to Killmonger even after the return of T'Challa. In this situation, the Wakandan army had a choice to follow the individual who had legitimate power (Killmonger) or the one who had referent power (T'Challa).

The final form of power is the one that leadership researchers suggest we use least often but it's often used by villains in the MCU: coercive power. Coercive power is a step beyond reward power where the individual forces people to do something against their will. An example of this in Black Panther is when Killmonger, after receiving the herb that provides him with his superpowers, burns the garden of herbs. He forces the priestesses to do that against their wishes. In your own experiences in the workplace, you may have seen situations where a toxic leader forced employees to do things against their will. Leadership researchers do not recommend using this form of power very often. It can have negative effects on employee job satisfaction (Faiz, 2013).

Unchecked coercive power can become a long-term form of toxic leadership known as abusive supervision. Abusive supervision can be seen in a variety of villainous leaders in the MCU. The leader of the Ten Rings terrorist organization can be seen as an abusive supervisor, forcing many of their team members to do things against their wishes. Killmonger coerces the Dora Milaje to the point that they choose to rebel against him. Coercion is often about satisfying a leader's needs above those of their followers (we'll discuss more about followers and leaders in Chapter 11).

## When Leadership Pipelines Go Awry

One important issue that many organizations face as they select leaders has to do with how their leadership selection systems work. McEntire and Green-Shortridge (2011) note that if leadership pipeline systems malfunction, the organization may face negative results. Maintaining these systems requires reflection on how and why decisions are made. A good example of malfunctioning systems involves why Killmonger was given an opportunity to become the Black Panther. A patrilineal royal succession process that involves challenges to a primary contender may not be the best method by which to choose the next king. Each step of Wakanda's royal selection process succumbs to poor planning. Reopening the challenge process for Killmonger may be correct on the face of the rules, but the results are far from positive. Succession planning processes must be applied fairly and consistently, but the ultimate goal of finding the best leader must not be lost in the name of these processes. The malfunctioning systems in Wakanda almost lead to Wakanda's science and technology being deployed against the rest of the world.

For an organization to correct itself during a malfunctioning leadership succession process, individual employees must work together to correct the situation. When Killmonger is wrongly given the title of Black Panther, Shuri, Ramonda, and Nakia must look to the next best choice to serve as Black Panther. They turn to M'Baku who despite opposing T'Challa is an honorable man. This represents the referent power that M'Baku has in relation to other potential candidates. M'Baku helps to heal T'Challa and help him regain the mantle of Black Panther. He chooses to do this despite disagreeing with T'Challa earlier. T'Challa has earned M'Bakus' respect based on his authenticity as a leader. T'Challa's choice to show mercy builds his referent power and pays off when seeking M'Baku's help.

When thinking of your own actions in your organization, it can be beneficial to think in terms of power. What power sources do you have access to? Which bases of power will help you in your goals as a leader? Power is useful and can help move you into a leadership position even if you don't have a formal title yet. Leadership covers many different aspects of one's work, and each portion of your work may provide you with bases of power whether it's your relationships, your knowledge, or your formally assigned activities. T'Challa uses all the bases of power to his advantage to defeat Killmonger. Killmonger focuses on coercive and legitimate power above all else. Imagine a coworker who focuses on the abilities that the formal job description provides and does nothing beyond that. Killmonger works that way as a leader. T'Challa sees a much larger picture and uses his relationships, knowledge, and reward abilities to motivate his followers to help him win back the throne.

## Summary

In this chapter, we reviewed the importance of building leadership pipelines. First, we focused on having leadership talent within your organization by recruiting effective leaders. We cannot develop high-potential leaders without talented individuals. We also focused on identifying high-potential individuals who had the skills necessary to be leaders. We especially focused on using objective assessments of leadership skill to identify high-potential leaders. Objective assessments not only help organizations identify high-potential leadership talent but also help to reduce bias. Reducing bias helps organizations level the playing field and provide opportunity to employees regardless of demographic characteristics (i.e., gender, race/ethnicity). Those high-potential leaders should then be provided learning opportunities to develop their leadership capabilities. A formal, clear process is one that is most effective when developing leaders for the future.

When attempting to select a leader, the source of a leaders' power is especially important. We discussed six bases of power in this chapter. Legitimate leadership refers to the leadership responsibilities provided by a formal job description. Reward power refers to the rewards that an individual can provide through their role. Information power refers to the information that a leader has that can be shared or not shared with others. Referent power refers to the affective feeling followers have for a leader. Expert power refers to leadership derived from one's knowledge of a subject matter. Coercive power refers to the ability of leaders to force subordinates to do their bidding. These bases of power can serve as reasons for a leader to be chosen over another.

Chapter 3

# Who Leads This Motley Crew? Shared and Team Leadership in the Guardians of the Galaxy

Superhero teams are often faced with a problem of power. Individual heroes who are powerful enough to headline their own film are asked to join forces with one another to battle even larger threats. The Avengers join forces to battle enemies greater than any single hero could handle. In the *Guardians of the Galaxy* films, we see a similar dynamic with our misfit band of spacefaring heroes. When a group of powerful (or skilled) individuals join a team, there can be some difficulty in managing leadership. In some cases, there's a battle for power and leadership on the team.

Teams of talented individuals often participate in shared leadership. In this chapter, we'll talk about how teams can benefit from shared leadership. We will discuss how teams' function under the guidance of a leader and interact with each other as a group and with other teams as a formal unit. Finally, we'll talk about how to make your team thrive using shared and team leadership theories!

## We are a Team

Teams are a common part of our work lives and the Marvel Cinematic Universe (MCU). As organizations move to flatter structures, teams have become the basic building blocks of organizational functioning (Randall, Resick, & DeChurch, 2011). Many organizations use distributed teams that do not work in the same geographic location but are distributed in a variety of physical locations and communicate using communications technologies. Teams are built of members who have a variety of competencies that can help teams address larger, more complex problems. Teams generally make better decisions, utilize resources more effectively, and become more creative (Ilgen, Major, Hollenbeck, & Sego, 1993). Organizations know that teams are effective; the question remains how do we develop this effectiveness?

An important factor that is often overlooked in forming a team is making a team feel like they are an actual unit or a team. For a team to be effective, they

Leaders Assemble! Leadership in the MCU, 17–23
Copyright © 2022 by Gordon B. Schmidt and Sy Islam
Published under exclusive license by Emerald Publishing Limited
doi:10.1108/978-1-80117-670-520221003

must perceive themselves as real (not just individuals who happen to work in the same area). A real team must meet three criteria: (a) clear boundaries for membership, (b) task interdependence, and (c) membership stability. Teams must recognize one another as a cohesive unit, understand a shared goal, and achieve a sense of who their members are. Without these traits, a team is not truly a team (Wageman, Hackman, & Lehman, 2005).

Marvel superheroes know how important teamwork is, though it may be difficult to get them to see themselves as part of a team. Even in solo adventures, heroes may team up with one another. The challenge is that many Marvel heroes are used to handling their villains on their own. Heroes need to know when and how they might team up to form a more powerful team capable of handling larger issues. This is a concern in Guardians of the Galaxy among each member of the potential Guardians team. Peter Quill (aka Star Lord) sees himself as a dashing, individual rogue even though he works with the interstellar Ravagers. Gamora is trying to get out of an unwilling team membership with her adopted father, Thanos. Drax the Destroyer sees only his mission of revenge for his lost family. Groot and Rocket see each other as partners but do not see a need for a larger team. These are all distinct individuals with their own goals and powers who must see each other as a team to be successful.

The Guardians of the Galaxy begin their journey as a team by being forced to work together in an intergalactic prison. Just like teams that you may have been a part of in your own work, there was some initial resistance to the idea of working together. Rocket and Gamora are used to doing things on their own. Rocket can plan an escape and repair weaponry on his own. But to escape the prison, Rocket realizes that he needs Star Lord, Gamora, and Drax. Each member of the Guardians recognizes that they need each other to accomplish a shared goal of escaping. A real team is formed once a team realizes it is a team. After the prison break, the Guardians of the Galaxy become a real team. The Guardians have multiple shared tasks (i.e., escaping prison, stopping Ronan the Accuser, stealing back the infinity stone), and they have determined their core membership. While developing a team may seem counterintuitive to leadership, you can't lead a team that doesn't see itself as a team.

Once a team identity has been established, a team leader can begin to develop or follow a leadership style. This process varies from organization to organization. In some organizations, a formal leader is authorized. In the MCU, we see this type of leadership in the form of Nick Fury and General Thaddeus "Thunderbolt" Ross. Both Fury and Ross serve in military organizations and have formal appointments as leaders with a formal title (i.e., Colonel). As we discussed in Chapter 2, formal leadership appointments come with formal power. Not only does Nick Fury inspire his followers (like Agent Coulson), but he has specific powers associated with the title Director of SHIELD. In a formal command and control organization such as SHIELD or General Ross' US state department military teams, there is little concern about who serves as leader, that is clearly delineated. But not all teams have such a strong level of hierarchy.

In Guardians of the Galaxy, we see the beginnings of a team of powerful equals. The initial fight on Xandar between the Guardians members indicates how evenly matched the team members are in terms of power. During the chase for the infinity stone before their capture, each team member shows their different skills and how they can neutralize the others' capabilities. Rather than a clear victor in this initial battle, the Guardians of the Galaxy are captured by the Nova Corps.

Teams work together in a variety of ways and require a unique leadership process. The Hill model of team leadership can help us to better understand how teams' function (Zaccaro, Rittman, & Marks, 2001). The Hill model proposes that leadership decisions in teams are often based on internal actions around tasks and relationships and external actions focused on dealing with the team's external environment. We'll discuss more about the external actions in Chapter 9, but for this chapter let's focus on the leaders' internal team decisions. In the model, a leader decides based on monitoring the internal activities of the team as well as the external environment. Based on how the leader views a particular problem or issue they may choose to focus on task-oriented behaviors or relationship-oriented behaviors and may respond to some changes in the external environment. Task-oriented behaviors are ones that are focused on the work of the team and often involves decision-making, maintaining standards, goal focusing, and structuring for results. Relational behaviors include actions that are meant to help team relationships such as coaching, collaboration, conflict management, and building commitment. These activities maintain the social environment where team performance can occur. These are all actions taken to help a team perform a task more effectively. These choices ultimately lead to team effectiveness. Team effectiveness is defined in terms of team performance (i.e., outcomes of the team) and team maintenance (i.e., continuing the team). This model tends to view leadership behavior as focused on team-based problem-solving. Leaders make important decisions about how to approach a problem based on the choices they make. Their choice of what to focus on to maintain the team or to help their team perform more effectively has a major impact on team effectiveness.

An example of the team leadership model in Guardians of the Galaxy is during the discussion of what the Guardians should do as they search for the Infinity Stone. At one point, Rocket becomes very angry because he is referred to as vermin. This comment is very offensive to him. Star Lord can evaluate this situation and chooses to focus on interpersonal relationships in the team. In the Hill model, we would refer to this as a relational action. Star Lord takes the time to validate Rocket and make it clear to him that Rocket is not vermin. Star Lord spends time calming him down and making Rocket feel better and like a real member of the team. Star Lord uses his interpersonal skills to help Rocket feel like a member of the team. We see a similar interaction when the Avengers fight the Chitauri during the Battle of New York. Captain America takes charge during this scenario and focuses on the important team tasks that each Avenger must focus on. Notice that each correct action depends on the leader understanding what's needed for their team to succeed in these situations. In some cases, teams need to be told what to do (like being told to go find a shawarma place), and in other cases, they need to build on their relationships (while eating shawarma).

In your own work, you may see that your teams require your leaders to behave in different ways depending on the problem. In many cases, leaders must help team members refocus on the task at hand. A good leader must clarify the role of an individual on their team. During the *Avengers* films, when a character needs clarification they know they can turn to Captain America or Iron Man to help guide their actions. However, leadership isn't just about getting things done. Maintaining a team, especially an effective one within your organization means having strong relationships. Many of us can recount times where we have had bosses who were so focused on the task at hand that they did not manage relationships effectively. In other situations, a leader may value relationships too much. In the Hill model of leadership, the leader's evaluation of the situation determines where the leader places their focus, either on tasks or relationships. When you serve as a leader on your teams, you will also need to make a determination about what approach is needed given your team's current needs.

## We Share Leadership

Superhero teams are often comprised of highly competent members capable of managing their own tasks. However, when a superhero team forms, it's usually to battle a larger than life villain that a single hero can't tackle on their own. The Avengers initially form to face Loki and an alien army. The Guardians of the Galaxy form to stop Ronan the Accuser from helping Thanos gain an Infinity Stone. Each team is comprised of members who have high-level competencies. These competencies are necessary to win a battle against a major foe. Strong teamwork is essential to these teams' successes. A group of high performers don't always need a clearly designated leader but need clearly designated competencies. This division of competencies requires a leadership approach that is referred to as shared leadership, which we discussed briefly in the first chapter. Shared leadership is defined as distributed leadership influence shared across team members (Carson, Tesluk, & Marrone, 2007). This type of shared influence can only occur with team members who have similar teamwork competencies and unique situational skill sets. Each team member has their own specialty and can be called upon to do different types of work that fit with that specialty. When dealing with a team without a clear command and control structure and evenly matched members, shared leadership may be the best team leadership approach.

Teams are often described as a leadership substitute. A substitute for leadership is anything that reduces the dependence of the follower on a leader (Schriesheim, 1997). Substitutes serve in place of leadership to fulfill a similar function. Leadership substitutes are used in situations where a formal leader is not necessarily in place. Self-managed teams that are autonomous often do not have a formal assigned leader and tend to function through the process of shared leadership.

The Guardians of the Galaxy present a compelling example of shared leadership and teamwork. Each member of the Guardians of the Galaxy serves in a leadership capacity at different points in time. This is a team of equals with no one as the clear leader despite efforts at times from Star Lord and Rocket to be the one leader. Leadership in the moment is determined by the teams' needs at a given time. When the Guardians team is initially forming, Star Lord persuades Drax to join their team along with Gamora. Despite Drax's hatred for Gamora, Star Lord convinces his team member to join them in an escape from prison.

After the team is formed, the Guardians experience their first leadership role change. Rocket takes center charge as the one who can break them free from the prison. He lays out the plan that the Guardians will use to escape. The team members recognize his expertise and defer to his knowledge to lead them out of the prison. Rocket specifies everyone's role, and they move forward with the plan (albeit unexpectedly due to Groot's jumping the gun on the steps of the plan). As individual contributors, each team member can be effective once they are given a task. This team doesn't need a lot of supervision and can act on the tasks to help Rocket complete his plan.

The leadership role then switches once the Guardians are on their way to Kno-where to meet with the Collector. Gamora focuses on the task and tells the Guard-ians they need to wait until they can meet the Collector. Star Lord focuses on the relationships of the team. He mends the relationship between Drax and Rocket during their bar fight by focusing on their need for quality friendships within the team. After the Guardians are attacked on Knowhere, Star Lord switches his focus to the task of getting the stone and Gamora back. Star Lord directs Rocket to use the pods to keep Nebula and her minions at bay while Star Lord can save Gamora. In each of these situations, we see leadership moving from individual contributor to individual contributor.

The level of shared leadership among the Guardians is especially apparent right at the end of their first adventure together. They sit in a circle to discuss what they should do about Ronan the Accuser and the Infinity Stone after they lose it. Shared leadership can help teams manage conflict and make decisions more effectively (Bergman, Rentsch, Small, Davenport, & Bergman, 2012; Hu, Chen, Gu, Huang, & Liu, 2017). Since the team does not have a clear leadership structure, there is a high level of conflict during their discussion of what to do about Ronan and the Infinity Stone. Star Lord appeals to their shared loss and focuses on their relationships to build consensus around his plan. Star Lord uses authentic leadership behaviors, specifically an internalized moral perspective, to guide the Guardians to the right choice. Teams that share leadership need to be able to manage conflict, and the Guardians of the Galaxy exhibit this behav-ior when it counts. Together, the Guardians make the right decision and choose to work with their teammates to make a final stand against Ronan the Accuser. This is only possible through healthy team relationships and Star Lord's authentic leadership behaviors.

Shared leadership can occur when an individual team member exhibits leader behaviors. Among the Guardians of the Galaxy, this sometimes results in surprising members showing leadership capabilities. When all seems lost in the Guardians mission against Ronan, it is Groot who declares to the Guardians "We are Groot," indicating that they are all part of one group and identifying the Guardians of the Galaxy as a true team. It's Groot's sacrifice that brings the team together. Research on authentic leadership (George, Sims, McLean, & Mayer, 2007) indicates that authentic leaders genuinely want to serve others. Groot's sacrifice is a form of authentic leadership and helps to bring the team together to face Ronan. Even Drax the Destroyer is able to show how much confidence he has in Mantis when they face Ego. Drax articulates his belief in her ability to help against their Celestial enemy. This is a common leader behavior and helps to build capacity for a follower to complete a task.

When the Guardians face Ronan on the surface of the planet Xandar, they also show a knack for shared leadership. Before Ronan begins to destroy the planet, both Star Lord and Rocket begin to work on their plans. Star Lord engages in dance shenanigans, while Rocket begins to build a weapon. Both are following Groot's lead and working as a team. When Gamora takes Star Lord's hand so that the Guardians can hold the Infinity Stone together, this is the final symbol of their shared leadership responsibility. The team views themselves as the Guardians of the Galaxy and have accepted each other as team members and potential leaders on missions moving forward.

Evidence of the Guardians' shared leadership can be seen when the Guardians are separated or work with other teams or groups. During their adventure with Ego, Star Lord articulates a vision for the mission against Ego's plan. While Rocket develops a plan to use explosives to destroy the Celestial. This is a pattern common to teams with shared leadership where a mission or vision is articulated quickly, and the team can implement it because their team members know how to manage both their relationships and their tasks effectively.

The Guardians prove to be an asset to the Avengers in Infinity War because of their adaptability. The Guardians split their forces by sending Rocket with Thor to develop a new hammer for the Asgardian, while Star Lord and the others support Iron Man, Spider-Man, and Dr Strange in their fight against Thanos. Despite what appears to be bickering, the Guardians of the Galaxy exemplify the effectiveness of shared leadership for self-managed teams.

As you can see, shared leadership means that leaders can be anyone on the team. Empowered employees can step up and show their leadership capabilities in a variety of ways. Shared leadership means that your team members can support one another, clarify tasks, provide information, and other forms of support. Strong teams with team members who are effective, individual contributors know how to manage one another. But these teams need a strong sense of identity, team trust, and conflict management skills. It takes time to develop a sense of team, but if you can provide your teams with a strong sense of shared purpose and a goal, that will help them to build shared leadership capabilities. Within your own organizations, you can develop stronger shared leadership or team leadership by focusing on building up the team coordination abilities. Develop a strong shared vision with clear roles for each team member. Make sure that the team knows how to work with one another to coordinate effectively. Establish strong norms for communication and sharing information. If you can do that, you have a team that can share leadership. Before your team can utilize a shared leadership method, your team must have the right mix of teamwork skills and individual competencies to manage your team within the organizational context.

## Summary

Leaders are important but so are teams. In some cases, teams can become autonomous and serve without a formal leader in place. The first step in building a team that can lead one another is to make them feel like they are a team. Effective team leadership requires a team identity that includes team interdependence, consistent team membership, and the recognition of all team members that they are a part of a team.

We used the Hill model of leadership (Zaccaro et al., 2001) to discuss how teams can more effectively work together by having internal activities within the team focused on task-oriented behaviors or relationship-oriented behaviors. A leader's choice to focus on task or relationship-oriented behaviors can have a major impact on the team's effectiveness. A good team leader needs to know when to use each of these techniques to maintain the team. Team leaders must be aware of what's happening within their team both in terms of the task and the team's relationships.

Finally, we discussed shared leadership where a team is autonomous and does not have a clearly delineated leader. In this situation, a team needs highly skilled members that also know how and when to coordinate activities. An autonomous team can only function when team members know how to deal with one another and are still highly skilled enough to complete necessary tasks. Teams that engage in shared leadership need to discuss and set boundaries around how work must be done to be effective.

Chapter 4

# With Great Power Comes Great Responsibility: Mentorship and Spider-Man

All heroes face challenges, but out of all the heroes in the Marvel Cinematic Universe, no one faces more consistent challenges balancing their superhero life and personal life than the friendly neighborhood Spider-Man: Peter Parker. With all the adversity Peter Parker (and those who wear a Spider-affiliated mantle) face, it's no wonder Spider-Man needs guidance. Whether it's at Peter Parker's Daily Bugle job, managing Stark's Iron Spider costume, or Miles Morales dealing with learning how to use his spider powers for the first time, all members of the Spider-Man family need guidance. This guidance often appears in the form of a mentor.

Leaders need mentors because it is often quite lonely in the position of leadership, just as it's lonely to be a superhero. Mentorship programs are one of the most common forms of leadership development in organizations (Kim, 2007). Research indicates that mentorship works (Eby, Allen, Evans, Ng, & DuBois, 2008) and can be used effectively in leadership development (Stead, 2005). In this chapter, we discuss how best to match mentors and mentees, how to manage a mentoring relationship, building a mentoring program, and how to build a shared vision among mentors and mentees through peer or group mentoring.

## With Great Mentors, Comes Great Leadership

Mentors are defined as individuals who have been where you wish to go in your career and who can serve as a guide and friend along that path (Reece & Brandt, 1993). Mentors serve two important purposes for future leaders: (a) they model career development behaviors and (b) they provide psychosocial support to their mentee (or protégé) (Kram, 1985). These two behaviors can be found in the relationship Peter has with Tony Stark. Tony Stark serves as an aspirational figure for Peter since he is the billionaire owner of a technology company. He can provide insight into Peter's future. Tony's belief in Peter provides enormous emotional support. Even after Tony Stark has died, Peter still turns to him for advice and

Leaders Assemble! Leadership in the MCU, 25–31
Copyright © 2022 by Gordon B. Schmidt and Sy Islam
Published under exclusive license by Emerald Publishing Limited
doi:10.1108/978-1-80117-670-520221004

guidance. As Peter goes through the process of becoming an Avenger, Tony Stark provides emotional support as well. Peter Parker's journey to becoming a hero truly began after he ignored the lessons from his greatest mentor, his uncle: Ben Parker. Ben's words about the responsibility that comes with power don't resonate with Peter until he loses Ben. One of the challenges for leaders or those who wish to become leaders is taking the time to listen to their mentors and accept their guidance. But why would someone like Peter Parker ignore the advice of his mentor and father figure? Especially considering the physical changes he experiences as Spider-Man? To understand this phenomenon, we must look at what makes a good match for a mentor and a protégé.

To build an effective mentor–protégé relationship, we must consider mentor matching. When protégés view their mentors as more like them, they perceive the relationship more positively (Mitchell, Eby, & Ragins, 2015). After Peter first receives his powers, he can't see his Uncle Ben as being similar any longer and disregards the advice of his mentor. As Peter continues his journey as a superhero, he often finds other mentors like Doctor Octopus and Tony Stark with whom he has mentorship relationships. In the case of Stark and Doctor Octopus, Peter sees a fellow scientist with whom he can relate. How might we identify potential mentors for potential protégés?

Bozeman and Feeney (2008) proposed a Goodness-of-Fit model of Mentor Matching. Their model breaks up the one-on-one relationship between mentor and protégé into three distinct parts, each serving a goal of the mentor or protégé. The first part of the relationship is referred to as endowments. Endowments represent what the mentor and mentee bring to the relationship. The mentor's endowments include knowledge of the workplace, work experience, and their social capital and ability to communicate. In other words, is the mentor respected in the workplace and are they someone that can provide relevant information to the protégé. Protégés' endowments include communication ability, learning ability, and knowledge. In other words, can the protégé learn and communicate effectively during the mentoring relationship? When Peter Parker meets Captain America for the first time, Peter immediately shows respect for him, indicating that he would be open to a mentoring relationship (despite taking the Captain's shield from him). We see a similar reaction from Peter Parker when he meets Doctor Otto Octavius prior to his transformation into the villainous Doctor Octopus. Peter opens the door to mentorship from Octavius by making it clear that he knows that Octavius' knowledge, both personal and scientific, are of value to him.

The second part of the relationship is known as preferences. Preferences have to do with the desire to be in the mentoring relationship. For mentors, preferences are affected by whether there is value in sharing their knowledge with others. For protégés, the question is whether they are willing to receive this knowledge from others. We see a disconnect between a mentor's desire to mentor and a protégé's willingness to learn in "Into the Spider-Verse," where Peter B. Parker is unwilling to serve as Miles Morales' mentor. Miles can't wait to learn what it means to be Spider-Man from the alternate universe Peter Parker. But Peter B. Parker has little desire to take on a protégé, and this blocks their mentoring relationship. A similar disregard is seen between Peter Parker and Uncle Ben. Peter can't see what

Uncle Ben might know of real power, given Ben Parker's lack of superpowers. It isn't until Peter loses Ben that he can see the value of his mentor's words.

The third part of the mentor–protégé relationship is the content of the relationship. Content refers to what is shared in this social exchange. Protégés and mentors are both capable of benefitting from this knowledge exchange. A protégé receives knowledge about how best to navigate their career while a mentor may receive valuable knowledge about the state of the organization from a protégé. While we imagine that mentorship is a one-way street, the research indicates that mentorship has benefits that go in both directions. We see the importance of content in the relationship between Peter B. Parker and Miles Morales. Peter B. Parker has little interest in mentoring, but as a visitor in an alternate universe, he does see the value in Miles taking him to his favorite burger spot. Miles sees a potential learning experience but becomes frustrated when he realizes Peter B. Parker isn't ready to hold up his end of the agreement. Both parties must be committed to the mentoring relationship for it to work.

The mentor matching model also highlights why conflict occurs between Tony Stark and Peter Parker during their mentoring relationship. In "Far From Home," Tony and Peter have an emotional discussion after Peter's friends were almost hurt. Tony sees much of Peter in himself and explains that he's trying to stop Peter from making the same mistakes. Peter accuses Tony of not listening because he's just a kid. In this situation, if Tony paid more attention to the content of Peter's words, and was able to communicate more effectively and listen, together they could have solved the problem.

What can we learn from this model of mentor matching? First, that finding the right mentor may take some time. Finding someone with the right mix of endowments, preferences, and context can be difficult. But as you search for a new mentor, it's important that you develop your own endowments. As you begin the journey of becoming a leader, understand that you should have the requisite knowledge to bring to your mentorship relationship. This model clearly delineates how mentorship is a two-way street. The process must be valuable for both parties for the mentoring to be successful. If you are currently a leader considering taking on a mentor, it's important to consider the value you bring and what you may receive from a protégé. Many mentors receive insights about current events or office politics within their organizations while sharing their insights and developing the next generation of leaders.

## Don't Do it Like Me, Do it Like You

The relationship between mentor and protégé can be affected by multiple factors. Research shows us that one major factor is perceived similarity, especially around demographic characteristics. Ensher and Murphy (1997) indicated that racial similarity impacted how much protégés enjoyed the mentoring relationships and increased contact between a mentor and protégé. Identifying mentors who match protégés in terms of race can be helpful to protégés as they progress through the process of leadership development. However, even racially matched pairs of mentors and mentees are not a guaranteed fit. In "Into the Spider-Verse,"

Miles thinks his father Jefferson is not a good fit as a mentor and prefers his uncle Aaron. As Miles learns more about Jefferson and Aaron, he begins to understand the differences between the two brothers and what makes Jefferson a better mentor and role model. The lesson here is that it's not enough to have demographic level matching, but demographics can have an impact on how mentor–protégé relationships play out. In leadership development, there may be insights that can be shared between mentors and protégés of similar backgrounds. Shared experiences can deepen the relationship between the mentor and protégé. One of the defining characteristics of the Spider-People in "Into the Spider-Verse" is that they all have the shared experience of lost loved ones. This is a bond that brings them all together.

For a mentor, these similarities can be helpful in guiding their protégé. Despite his initial hesitation with the role of mentor, Tony Stark is a strong mentor for Peter Parker. As he works with Peter, Tony strikes to protect him from the mistakes he's made in the past by providing him insight into what it means to be a hero. We see a similar arc with the experience between Miles and Peter B. Parker. Despite the initial hesitation with the role of mentor, Peter B. Parker finds the commonality between himself and Miles to help guide Miles through the initial stages of becoming Spider-Man. While demographic similarity may be important, it is the shared vision of mentorship goals that provides the most impact in a high-quality mentor–protégé relationship.

Research has indicated that demographic characteristics can have an impact on the quality of the mentoring relationships between mentor and protégé; however, what matters the most to mentees is an overlap of relevant knowledge (Carapinha, Ortiz-Walters, McCracken, Hill, & Reede, 2016). When developing a relationship with a mentor or serving as a protégé, highlight the commonalities especially around knowledge. Make sure that the endowments in the relationship are clear so mentor and protégé can get the most out of the relationship. As a mentor, you can impact your relationship with a protégé by highlighting similarities and trying to meet the protégé from a place of understanding and care.

Despite the importance of similarity between mentors and protégés, differences can be valuable as well. Research has indicated that men and women provide different values in mentoring, with male mentors more providing more career development support and women spending more time on socioemotional material (O'Brien, Biga, Kessler, & Allen, 2010). This gender divide can be seen in the mentorship Miles receives from Aunt May which focuses on the grief that she feels in losing her Peter Parker as well as the emotions Miles feels in losing his uncle Aaron. Miles' father, Jefferson, has a harder time with the emotional content of mentorship as evidenced by his difficulty in communicating with Miles from beyond his dorm room door. Jefferson is much comfortable in the squad car dispensing career-oriented advice about how Miles can do well in his private school. But both mentors are key individuals in Miles' development of his leadership skills. Different mentors may provide different types of support. We'll discuss this again when we talk about peer mentoring.

One common theme in the examples of Spider-Man that we have seen in this chapter is the sense of hesitation. Many senior leaders seem hesitant to become mentors. Some leaders may see it as a waste of time, others may feel that they don't have much to offer the next generation of leaders. For those leaders who may be hesitant or those protégés looking to convince a leader to be their mentor, research has shown positive career impact on participating in mentorship programs. Leaders who participate in formal mentoring programs generally have greater career success, increased job satisfaction, and increased organizational commitment. Mentors gain as much as they give from formal mentoring programs. For organizations that are considering instituting a formal mentoring program, results indicate value for both mentors and protégés (Ghosh & Reio, 2013).

A formal mentoring program is a mentorship program supported by an organization. Many organizations develop formal mentoring programs for their leaders. To join a formal mentorship program, one must first excel in one's job. If you are looking to join a mentorship program you have to show that you have what it takes to do the work. Spider-Man proves to his multiple mentors (Tony Stark, Otto Octavius, Peter B. Parker, Jefferson) that he is worth the time to mentor. Effective mentoring programs usually target specific skills and behaviors while still providing emotional support. As a mentor, you must provide both career-related information and socioemotional knowledge. Mentoring in the leadership development process is about relationships. You can start to learn to be a leader by building the relationship with a potential mentor. When the opportunity arises to learn leadership skills from a Tony Stark or a Peter B. Parker, you should jump at the chance. Whether serving as a mentor or protégé, make sure to clarify what your goals are for the mentoring experience.

## Mentoring Among Peers

Learning how to be a leader doesn't just happen between a more experienced colleague and a less experienced colleague. Leadership development can also occur between peers. Peer mentoring is defined as a more collegial mentoring relationship between individuals of equal status (Cornu, 2005). Peer mentoring is often used with youth programs to help develop young people into leaders (Andrews & Clark, 2011). Peer mentoring programs have grown in popularity in organizations because managers are often overwhelmed and have less time to provide the guidance to develop new leaders (Holbeche, 1996).

In "Spider-Man: Into the Spider-Verse," we see a strong example of peer mentorship. While Peter B. Parker is ostensibly Miles' mentor, Miles also receives support and knowledge from the other Spider-People in the group. All of the heroes in "Into the Spider-verse" (Spider-Man: Noir, Spider-Gwen, Peni Parker, Spider-Ham) have more experience than Miles Morales, and each provides invaluable expertise and insight into his experiences as Spider-Man. Gwen has an especially strong relationship with Miles. In Miles, Gwen sees the friend she lost in her own world and immediately sees the value of the mentoring relationship that she might have with him.

Peer mentoring relationships can work because there is greater similarity between peers rather than leaders within organizations. Peer mentors can speak to each other more openly about situations without as great an understanding gap. In some cases, peer mentoring is also done as group mentoring. Group mentoring is defined as a mentoring relationship between more than two individuals (Huizing, 2012). Group mentoring has been shown to have beneficial effects on career advancement and the development of leadership skills (Sheinfeld Gorin, Lee, & Knight, 2020). The group of Spider-People in "Into the Spider-Verse" consistently support one another in a group mentoring format. Each member of the group has something to contribute to their development. It is through the encouragement of the group that Peter B. Parker becomes a stronger mentor and a mentor for Miles Morales. Spider-Ham, Spider-Gwen, Peni Parker, and Spider-Man: Noir are all able to provide emotional support to one another when sharing their origin stories. Each of these alternate Spider-People has had similar experiences with losing someone and that sharing process in a group mentoring format provides solace to the characters. Their different perspectives help shed light on Miles' struggles as the newest individual to wear the mantle of Spider-Man. By mentoring Miles together, the Spider-People help Miles Morales take the "leap of faith" that he needs to become his own Spider-Man.

Group mentoring can also help leaders develop a shared vision. Leaders who serve as informal mentors on their teams, or peers who serve as mentors to others can build a shared vision. This is form of sensemaking (which we'll discuss more in Chapter 9). The process of mentorship can help leaders develop a shared vision with their team members or with others in their organization. Group mentoring helps to facilitate that process further. When working with a group of peers, you can build a common idea by maintaining consistent communication (Farmer, Slater, & Wright, 1998). Consistent communication between mentors and protégés is a key factor in the quality of a mentoring relationship both among groups and individual mentors. Through the group mentoring process, this group of alternate universe dwellers can create a shared vision for their final plan. They build consensus while supporting one another. Even when the plan needs to change, their shared concept of what the goal must be helps the group succeed in sending all the Spider-People home.

This process of communication, growth, and trust among peers with Miles eventually emerging as a leader in his own right can be seen in the various action scenes in "Into the Spider-Verse." As the story progresses, Miles goes from being an observer in various battles, to being a key contributor in the final battle. He grows over time through communication processes with his peer mentors like Spider-Gwen. His peer mentors share invaluable advice about using their powers. Peter B. Parker serves as a more senior mentor providing him with an overall scope of who Miles is and who Miles can become. Peter B. Parker helps to create a framework for Miles' development.

What does that mean for you as you work through peer, group, or individual mentorship? First, try to find a mentor who matches you in terms of career planning, goals, or communication style. Find a mentor that can help you become the leader you wish to be. Second, take advantage of your peers. As you move through the leadership development pipeline, it is in your best interest to reach out to your peers who are developing their leadership skills along the same path that you are. The more you build those relationships, the more effective the mentoring process will be. The classical definitions of leadership often break up leadership into two foci: task and relationship. Thus, mentoring relationships are an effective way to develop your relationship building skills as you become take on the great power of leadership.

## Summary

In this chapter, we discussed the importance of mentorship for leadership development. Mentors can provide valuable insight to future leaders, and the mentoring process can be beneficial to both mentors and protégés. One key factor in a mentoring relationship is matching appropriate mentors with protégés so that there is a mutual respect based on knowledge, social capital, and potential for career advice. Good mentorship is a two-way street where mentors and protégés can each benefit from each other's knowledge and social support. If an organization doesn't have the resources for one-on-one mentors, group or peer mentoring can provide a useful alternative. To maximize the benefit from these relationships, you should try to increase communication among mentors and protégés and focus on building effective relationships that can lead to growth in leadership skills. Mentors and protégés can work together to build a shared vision for their team. Becoming a mentor or a protégé just takes a leap of faith.

Chapter 5

# How Do Leaders (Superheroes or Not) Deal with Conflict?

When we think of conflict in Marvel Cinematic Universe (MCU) films, our mind probably first goes to the epic physical conflicts between heroes and villains. And while the Marvel films are full of such fights, we often see many nonphysical conflicts, even among the heroes. Heroes in Marvel films often have their own unique perspectives and opinions, which can bring them into conflict with others, even with other heroes they may share many goals with.

A great example of this is found in "Captain America: Civil War" as the Avenger team comes into conflict (and even later physical blows) about the future of the team and how it will function and make decisions. Should the team be led by the agenda of an international organization or should it continue as a team where the members make their own decisions? We see major team leaders Captain America and Iron Man disagree on this, and the team is ultimately torn apart related to this conflict and others.

This chapter will look at the nature of this conflict and others in the Avengers team to help us think about how we, as leaders, can best handle the conflicts in our own teams and relationships. We will talk about how researchers have looked at and defined different kinds of conflict and that researchers have found that some conflict is actually good for teams. People also differ in their conflict management responses, with collaboration often the best path to a good solution. We'll help you to be a leader who can better deal with conflict and successfully negotiate your issues with others, superheroes or not.

## When Titans Clash! (Or Work Colleagues Disagree)

Conflict can be seen as tension that arises between members of a team (like the Avengers) when there are differences of opinion or values (De Dreu & Weingart, 2003). Team members, thus, can disagree on what actions the team should take, the appropriate values to have, and even how members of the team should behave.

When researchers look at types of conflict, they generally find two big categories: task conflict and relationship conflict. Task conflict focuses on what the team should do and how it should use its resources. So for a team like the Avengers,

Leaders Assemble! Leadership in the MCU, 33–38
Copyright © 2022 by Gordon B. Schmidt and Sy Islam
Published under exclusive license by Emerald Publishing Limited
doi:10.1108/978-1-80117-670-520221005

it might mean what the right strategy to defeat Loki is or how work should be divided, such as who should be in which subgroup for the tasks needed to defeat Thanos.

Relationship conflict, meanwhile, is about conflict people have with each other related to personal characteristics such as personal taste, values, and personal preferences for how to work with others (De Dreu & Weingart, 2003). So if Iron Man thinks that Captain America is too much of a "boy scout" and Captain America thinks Iron Man is too "cynical," we are talking about a relationship conflict.

While you might think that conflict in a team is always bad (i.e., "We don't want to fight!"), research finds that conflict can actually be helpful in some circumstances, generally when it involves task conflict. Task conflict involves team members discussing and determining how to do a task. These discussions can lead to the team coming up with a better result than if one person's idea was just followed, and researchers have found that task conflict can lead to greater creativity in a team (Lee, Avgar, Park, & Choi, 2019).

This makes sense if you think about the Avengers and what they do. When fighting a major threat like Thanos, a great plan is needed and no individual Avenger may have the full solution. Each Avenger brings their own experiences, skills, and opinions to the situation. By having them all speak, disagree, and have some conflict on what is the best course of action, a new, better, plan may come out. A plan might be mostly Iron Man's ideas but Hawkeye could add a valuable part to it that means success versus losing to Thanos.

So task conflict can be good! Should we strive for task conflict all the time? Well, as you might expect, disagreement at all times might not actually be good. While conflict on what to do related to a task can help lead to a more creative or better plans, at times task conflict can also lead to the other type of conflict we talked about, relationship conflict.

Relationship conflict has been found to generally hurt team performance and creativity (De Dreu & Weingart, 2003). So if we fight with each other related to our personalities and values it often will hurt our relationships with each other. How much do you trust a coworker you think is immoral or that you don't like as a person? Even if their skills are high and they have insight, it can be hard to act on that insight and believe them.

In the Avengers films, we can see the negative impacts of this in the relationship conflict between Captain America and Iron Man. They have values that can come into conflict. Captain America is more idealistic, he can be more likely to want to follow the rules, and when it is a moral question, he will not back down, as we see in "Captain America: Civil War." Iron Man meanwhile is quite cynical and sarcastic, willing to bend or break the rules, and willing to make compromises on moral issues. Working together on a task, these different perspectives might help to come up with a more creative and better solution. However, when they just fight with each other about their own different perspectives and values, they may not be able to come to a solution at all. When discussing if the United Nations should control the Avengers, Captain America and Iron Man are on different sides and feel the other one is unreasonable. They are not valuing the different perspective of the other one, rather just discounting the other perspective as wrong, faulty reasoning due to these different personal values. And as we see in the Marvel films from "Captain America: Civil War" onward, these personal differences make it very hard for the Avengers to work together and be the effective team they were in the past (or even be a team at all!).

So how might task conflict lead to relationship conflict? Think about your own experiences. If someone always disagrees with you, how might you feel about them? Oftentimes, we may feel frustrated at people we disagree with and that might lead us to feel negatively toward them. This is especially true if in task conflict discussion we end up clashing on values or personalities. When Captain America sees Iron Man as cynical, he may be discounting useful task information, thinking it is not important and just an illustration of Iron Man's personality. In such a situation, the relationship conflict could lead to the task conflict being ineffective.

Research suggests the majority of conflict is not at the group level, rather it is between individuals or in subgroups. Most conflict is two people in conflict with each other (Shah, Peterson, Jones, & Ferguson, 2021). So conflict is often between two people or in a subset of the overall group. And these conflicts can actually help performance, as Shah and colleagues (2021) found task conflict due to a difficult individual or two people in conflict related to higher team performance! It was only when the task conflict raised to the level where most people on the team had task conflict that such conflict was negative. As a leader, you may encourage some task conflict, but make sure it doesn't get to a level where everyone on the team is in disagreement with each other.

## Resolving Your Conflict Like a Hero (Or Even Just a Good Leader)

When people, superheroes or not, are in conflict, an ultimate decision needs to be made on what the team will do and how conflict will be resolved. The conflict management approaches used by leaders can be put into five major categories, depending on how assertive and cooperative a person's approach is (Volkema & Bergmann, 1995).

The first conflict management type is a "forcing" approach, with a leader just making others go along with their own preference. The leader is very assertive with little cooperation. This approach can be successful when the leader has high levels of power and control over what happens, but it can make others resentful and rarely makes them feel motivated toward the course of action (Whetten & Cameron, 2020). We can see Iron Man trying to use this approach when he reminds the Avengers he is the one paying for everything. He is essentially saying, "it is my money, we should do what I want." This approach is ineffective when a person doesn't have the authority or power to make others go along with it, as we see Captain America and some other Avenger not go along with the decision to have the United Nations (UN) control the group. They have the ability to refuse, and they do so in this case.

The second type we term as an "avoiding" approach, and in such a situation, a leader and others just avoid making a decision. The leader is low in assertiveness and cooperation. Have you ever had to make a difficult decision and just tried to ignore it for a while? That is what this approach essentially is. This approach is very ineffective in resolving a situation as no decision is made. If some other person or group will go ahead and make the decision if you don't, it does allow you to avoid taking the responsibility and blame for the decision. However, it makes it quite likely the ultimate result is worse for your own interests. If the Avengers had just ignored the pending deadline the UN set for its rules for the Avengers it would be the team taking this avoiding approach.

The third type we term as an "accommodating" approach, when a leader just goes ahead and does what the other person wants. This is a leader being high in cooperation but low in assertiveness. If you don't care what the result of a decision is (e.g., not caring where you go out to dinner), this can be a reasonable choice. However, it likely means you are not getting any aspect of what you actually want, which in the long term can lead to resentment and damaged relationships. So Captain America would have been engaging in accommodating had he just gone along with what Iron Man said related to the UN running the team, despite his own personal beliefs to the contrary.

The fourth conflict management type is a "compromising" approach when a discussion leads to people settling on a solution. This can be seen as a moderate level of cooperating and assertiveness. In compromising, each side gives up some of what they want to come up with a solution that is acceptable (Whetten & Cameron, 2020). If two people want the last remaining pizza slice so you cut it in half that is a clear illustration of this approach. Compromising can be a very helpful approach in that unlike other approaches you don't have one side "winning" and the other "losing." Each side gets some of what they want.

Where compromise can be not ideal at times is that to some degree neither party really gets a "win." A solution is decided on but to some degree it is not what either side in the conflict really wants. While a compromise is usually better for a relationship than the previous types, over time a person can begin to feel they just don't get what they want. We all need to compromise at times, but if we always have to do it, we can feel not listened to or not getting what we need or want. Compromise also has a tendency toward "splitting things down the middle." So instead of talking through the problem to figure out what is best, often we just give each side half or alternate the decision. So something like "you pick what we eat Monday, I pick what we eat Tuesday." The compromise is a decision made that includes both parties, but it may not be the best decision. In the case of the Avengers, perhaps a compromise would be if the UN controlled some aspects of the team (like mission assignment), then the team members controlled others things (like who can be a member of the team). The UN may have been willing to compromise on some aspects of team control, but they were never asked in the film itself (and bringing them into the discussion could have been very helpful!).

The fifth conflict management type is called "collaborating," where the parties in conflict talk through their different perspectives, needs, and goals. Collaboration can be the best method, as it involves working together to find a solution that truly meets the needs of both parties. Thus, this type can be seen as the only type that allows for a "win-win" result (Whetten & Cameron, 2020). This can work as while parties may seem to have oppositional desires, when their interests are more clearly understood and thought through new solutions are found. For example, two people may think they need a single car at the same time and that is a conflict, but when they actually compare their schedules, one person could be dropped off at a place (and thus could be driven there instead of retaining the car) or resources could be divided in a way that resolves the situation (the person who gets the car pays for the other person's Uber ride to their different destination). Collaboration allows for a better decision to be made that potentially meets both party's needs or at least meets needs better than a compromise would. The major drawback to this approach can be that good collaboration takes time and a willingness for everyone involved in the conflict to engage with others and share their interests. In some cases, you might have people who don't want to do that or don't trust the other party.

In the case of the conflict in the Avengers, we do not see collaboration happening in the film itself, but it could have. Collaboration would involve Captain America and Iron Man explaining in more detail why they held their particular positions and what their interests really were. It is possible that when this was all more clearly articulated, a solution could be found where there is the outside oversight Iron Man wants while there is also the amount of independence and ability to act on personal morals that Captain America values. For one potential solution, perhaps the UN generally assigned missions and offers oversight for the team (fitting Iron Man's perspective) but that that individual members can decline to work on missions that don't fit their morals, and Avenger members can also propose missions for the team to undertake as well (potentially fitting some of Captain America's concerns). Since the film did not have greater discussion of member perspectives on the issue, we can't know for sure what a collaborative approach would have resulted in.

Looking at the conflict about UN control in "Captain America: Civil War," we generally see a forcing approach being applied in the situation, with disastrous results. Both Iron Man and Captain America seem to think they can force the team to do what they personally prefer, when in fact that perspective leads to the group breaking apart. Some other team members give reasons for one side or the other, which could be seen as attempts at compromising. Some team members seem to be just going along with whatever is decided, which might suggest an accommodating approach. Overall, only two options are presented, rather than a more beneficial approach of looking for other decisions that might lead to a better result for the Avengers, the UN, and probably the world these heroes protect. The conflict is primarily between Iron Man and Captain America, but it does seem to rise to a team-level conflict, with the negative impacts on performance and team success found in the research of Shah et al. (2021). It is important for leaders to make sure task conflicts help the quality of the team decision and not become a team-level conflict or a conflict that hurts the relationships between people, as we see in this situation.

## Summary

Conflict is part of the job for any superhero, but it is also a common part of any workplace. There is no place in the world that is truly conflict-free. This chapter discussed the nature of conflict, types of conflict, the impact of conflict on a team, and different conflict management styles. This knowledge helps you to be a better leader, as you know ways to deal with conflict as well as what kind of conflict can help your team to be better.

As we discussed earlier, while conflict is inevitable in teams that is to some degree a good thing, as task conflict can actually help us to come up with better plans and decisions. The different perspectives and ideas different people bring can help us to reach our goal, whether it is to defeat Thanos or to create an effective employee engagement program.

Conflict, however, can be bad when it hurts the relationships between team members, as can be seen in "Captain America: Civil War" when Captain America and Iron Man are unwilling to listen to each other and work toward a shared solution. Leaders need to help reduce conflict that is relationship focused, as such conflict about personal characteristics and values often leads to hurt work relationships and people not working toward a common goal. Too much conflict of any kind can be bad for a team as well, as if the whole team is in conflict at the same time, it can be hard to accomplish our goals. A good leader needs to make sure task conflict is useful and help to reduce conflict that hurts relationships.

We also discussed how leaders can engage in different conflict management approaches. The best approach overall is collaboration, as people work together to understand each other's goals and perspectives to come up with a solution that meets both parties' needs. It may look like two people have opposite perspectives, but when we work to understand each other, we often find out a better solution can be found out. Collaboration can take a lot of time though, so there will be times when other approaches are most appropriate, with compromise often the best of the remaining perspectives.

As a leader, you will need to be able to deal with conflict well. This chapter helps you to consider how you will deal with conflict well, using that conflict for the good of your team. We may argue about how to save the day, but when we listen to each other, we can figure out the best way to save the day.

Chapter 6

# Leadership During Crisis and Stress: Leadership During Stressful Times Like Thanos' "One Snap"

Marvel heroes often have to fight for the fate of the world while putting themselves in potential mortal risk. While our heroes triumph in the end, their superhero battles have significant stress and negative consequences on them. Heroes suffer from extreme stress and strain, with Iron Man showing signs of post-traumatic stress disorder (Scarlet & Busch, 2016).

In our own world, crises and extreme situations can and do happen. The COVID-19 pandemic is a recent example of a situation of unanticipated crisis where the actions of leaders had a huge impact on how it was reacted to. When a crisis hits, we need leaders who can best respond to the situation and navigate it as needed. And there are still many stressful events, big and small, that happen in our lives.

In this chapter, we look at the impact of stress on leaders and how we can try to counteract it. We look at how leaders negotiate crises, with advice on how to do so successfully. We all want to be the leader in a crisis who is able to persevere and ultimately save the day for our subordinates and the world.

## Superheroes and Super Stress

Stress is a physical or psychological reaction people have to a situation or potential situation that is perceived to threaten something they value. So these threats or stressors generally are perceived as unpredictable and/or uncontrollable, which is part of the reason they are seen as threatening (Cohen, 1980; Harms, Crede, Tynan, Leon, & Jeung, 2017). Note here the wording of "perceived." Whether something is seen as a stressor will depend on how a person perceives it. Something I see as threatening and thus a stressor might be something that isn't of concern to you. The use of "potential situation" is relevant as well. A stressor doesn't have to be something that has happened already, it can be something you worry will happen. So if someone is worried they will be laid off that can be a significant stressor even though it hasn't happened yet. When stress is prolonged

Leaders Assemble! Leadership in the MCU, 39–44
Copyright © 2022 by Gordon B. Schmidt and Sy Islam
Published under exclusive license by Emerald Publishing Limited
doi:10.1108/978-1-80117-670-520221006

and at a high level, our physical and emotional resources get exhausted and we become unable to cope with it, leading to negative effects like lower job performance, lower satisfaction, leaving a job, and even increased drug and alcohol use (Harms et al., 2017).

When we talk about stressors there are four major types: time, encounter, situational, and anticipatory (Whetten & Cameron, 2020). Each type represents a different general situation or context that has been found to make people feel stressed.

Time stressors involve people perceiving too much work to accomplish in the time available. Time can be a limited resource, especially for leaders, and not having enough time causes us stress. We see superheroes often experiencing these types of stressors related to balancing their superhero life and their normal lives. In your own life, you may see this with people who are workaholics and have little time available for family and friends.

Encounter stressors are when stress arises from interactions with other people. Have you worked with difficult people before in an organization? When we work with others we do not trust or often get in conflict with, stress can result. We can see this in the Avenger films as trust breaks down between Captain America and Iron Man. They argue about who is the leader and what others should do. Their interactions become more negative and stressful, with them ultimately unable to work together.

Situational stressors come from the environments a person works and lives in. If we live or work in areas where there is danger to our physical and mental well-being (as we see with superheroes), these may be significant stressors. Research also finds that people feel greater stress when they are going through significant or rapid changes in their lives, even when a change might be seen as positive, due to requiring readjustment effort (Scully, Tosi, & Banning, 2000). Certainly, we see these situational stressors in the Marvel Cinematic Universe (MCU). If we consider just Tony Stark, major life events include being kidnapped, getting a life-threatening injury, having his home destroyed, having a child, and putting his life at risk against a wide range of villains. We would expect Stark to feel a great amount of stress.

Anticipatory stressors involve threatening events that have not occurred yet. These are the stress of events that could happen but have not happened yet. They can be impactful events, such as a layoff or the threat of a villain returning for vengeance or relatively small events such as making a mistake when giving a class speech (Whetten & Cameron, 2020). These depend on what events a person is worried about and how likely they think the event is to happen. We see an example of this in "Avengers: Endgame," with different Avengers more or less concerned about risking their lives to undo Thanos' snap. With Tony Stark having a family and a good life, he felt significantly more anticipatory stress of putting his life at risk.

## Fighting Stress Like a Superhero

So how can we help to reduce stress in our own lives and those we lead? First, it is important to note that stress isn't always bad, a moderate level of stress has been argued to be useful for keeping people motivated and taking action. Stress can help us to focus on a topic as important and in need of our attention and effort. However, as noted above, prolonged stress at a high level has major negative consequences (Harms et al., 2017). We see Thor's behavior in "Avengers: Endgame" showing this, as he abandons being a hero and other responsibilities, wallowing in food and drink. So we don't want stress to reach such a prolonged and high level.

There are three major categories of stress management strategies that we can use for ourselves or apply as a leader to help reduce stress in our followers. They vary in terms of effectiveness in the short term versus the long term and how much effort and time they take to do. We will be looking at Bruce Banner, the Hulk, for examples.

The first type is reactive strategies, which will be short-term solutions for a particular situation (Whetten & Cameron, 2020). So the stress of the moment is dealt with by reacting with a short-term solution. One common short-term solution is to put in extra time or effort in the moment to resolve the stressful situation. So if you have a big project due tomorrow, making a pot of coffee and staying up late to finish is a reactive strategy. You are taking action that resolves the current stressor event. However, this reactive action rarely helps in the future. If you stay up all night today you will likely end up tired tomorrow. You may fall behind on other work you need. Your health will suffer if you pull too many all-nighters. Reactive strategies are often the easiest to implement in the short term, require little lead time and learning, and require only action for a relatively short-term period of time. However, they do little to resolve general problems, just taking care of a particular situation.

We see reactive strategies taken by Bruce Banner across Avenger films. They generally involve him getting close to the anger or blood pressure level that turns him into the Hulk, and in the moment, he tries to stop that transformation. Banner will often try to calm himself when he feels a change coming. He may also try to find a location where him "hulking out" is less problematic. In these cases, he is doing a reactive strategy – how do I manage this current time I am turning into the Hulk. Can I still stop the process? If I turn into the Hulk, how can I minimize damage? The overall problem of turning into the Hulk is unaddressed, just resolving this current instance in the best way possible.

The second type is proactive strategies, which is coming up with strategies that help us better deal with stress in general. For these strategies, we are building skills that help us deal with stress whenever it arises (Whetten & Cameron, 2020). So, for example, if we develop strong time management skills, we should be better able to schedule our work and be as efficient as possible, helping to reduce time stressors. Learning a technique like yoga might help a person to be more calm and reduce how much stress wears on them. We might also use technology tools to help us like a phone app that manages our calendar or that reminds us to do our yoga practice. Proactive strategies develop your capacity to deal with stress in general by learning relevant skills or finding relevant technological solutions. That new skills or applications need to be learned means that proactive strategies don't work to help emergency or short-term stressors (if the report is due tomorrow, don't learn how to do yogi tonight before starting it!). Proactive strategies help you deal more successfully with stressful situations and react to them better, but they don't remove the stressors entirely. If you do indeed have more work than time to do it, even when you manage your time well, the proactive strategy cannot resolve the situation. You'll see our last stress management strategy, enactive, is focused on eliminating stressors.

Turning to Bruce Banner, we see some proactive strategies he has implemented related to his major stressor of turning into the Hulk. We see in the film "The Incredible Hulk" that he has a wristwatch that is like a smart fitness wearable, monitoring his blood pressure and warning him when it is getting high (and thus will soon turn into the Hulk). This device helps to better monitor his blood pressure and thus gives some early warning that he needs to take action to calm down. We also hear Banner talk about working on keeping calm in general in his life. So Banner is trying to develop skills that reduce the magnitude of stress he feels so he is less likely to get into the "danger zone" where he turns into the Hulk.

The last type of stress management strategies is called enactive strategies, and they are focused on removing sources of stress (Whetten & Cameron, 2020). With these strategies you are changing the environment itself and eliminating the stressor. So if a long commute is a major source of stress for you, an enactive strategy could be to move to live closer to your workplace. Or you could find a job closer to where you live. As you can see, both of these enactive strategies have the advantage of eliminating the stressor but will probably take considerable time and effort in most cases. They might require hard choices as well – should I leave a job I like because a long commute is so averse to my well-being? That is a decision that people will decide quite differently based on their own preference and perceived stressors. So enactive strategies offer the significant advantage of potentially removing the stressors entirely. With our other two types, we either dealt with the stressors in the short term or became better at dealing with stressors in general. Here they might no longer be a concern. So this is a long-term solution that is likely to take a lot of time and effort to make happen. It might have to involve changing your perceptions and determining what really matters. Perhaps at one point you were willing to do whatever it took to be the best in your field, but do you actually value that more than your family? Your health? Enactive strategies can potentially require these types of considerations as well.

Returning to Bruce Banner one more time, we see a clear enactive strategy of Banner integrating his two identities together, than of Banner and the Hulk. Note that this required a change of perspective by Banner, as he used to only see Hulk as a stressor and problem. By seeing Hulk as part of himself, he was able to find a middle ground position with this part of himself. In "Avengers: Endgame," we only see this intelligent Hulk, but the process of integrating Banner's two selves takes place during the five-year gap in the film. It is likely integrating his two selves took a long time and a lot of work. Our own enactive strategies are unlikely to be the same as Banner, but they may take a lot of hard work and consideration on our own part.

## Leading in Stress and Crisis

Leaders are both impacted by stress and impact the stress of their followers. Harms and colleagues (2017) found that leaders had a major impact on the stress level of followers. Stress led leaders to engage in more abusive and negative behaviors toward followers, increasing followers' own stress level. Stress also seemed to lead to damage in the relationship between leaders and followers.

The nature of a crisis fits with what can lead to high stress. A crisis is a change from the norm that is unexpected and often seen as unpredictable as it continues to unfold. We've seen this related to COVID-19, but it is also true for events like terrorist attacks or weather disasters. Such crises are usually threatening in nature, as they put people at risk both physically and economically. And in terms of stressors, there can be situational current stressors (such as lost access to needed resources) and anticipatory stressors (such as the concern of getting a severe case of COVID-19 in the future).

Thus, we may think that leaders can play particular important roles in helping to reduce stress or make it worse in crisis situations. Brandebo (2020) examined destructive leader behaviors during crisis, finding leaders can be too controlling, avoiding others input, and too focused on just their own well-being, not the needs of subordinates. Such leaders are not dealing well with the stress of the situation and having it impact their behaviors and performance. Subordinates suffer additional stress beyond the crisis due to their leader's behaviors.

We can see some of these issues in MCU films. In the face of Thanos' snap and the initial failure to reverse it, we see many of the Avenger's former leaders abdicate their responsibilities. Iron Man essentially quits, going off to live a normal life. Thor stops being a leader on the team or of his people. Captain America seems to move to helping people deal with grief, which is potentially positive but seems to take him away from hero work. Thus, in different ways we can see all three turning to their own well-being versus the good of the Avengers team. Black Widow ultimately needs to step up and become a leader during the five-year gap, helping to organize heroes and others during this time of crisis. It takes a new element, Scott Lang with a new idea to take back the snap, for the heroes to come back together and ultimately save the day.

So if even our heroes fail in crisis, how can we be leaders who help our organizations to weather a crisis? It is important to consider where you are at in the process. The best way to weather a crisis is to be prepared before it happens. This includes forward planning. What would we do if a particular crisis happened? While we might not know the exact details of a future crisis, we can prepare for general categories of crises (such as a product recall or power outage) that might happen in your own industry. For leaders and companies, it is also important to have built a strong reputation (Hargis & Watt, 2010). When a crisis happens, a trusted reputation means others will give you the benefit of the doubt and be more receptive to do what needs to be done. If subordinates already didn't trust a leader, a crisis will only make the relationship worse.

Once the crisis has actually hit, a leader needs to be very intentional in making sure their behaviors reduce stress. Clear communication is important, so that subordinates understand what is happening and what they need to do. This includes open and transparent communication whenever possible (Lacerda, 2019). During COVID-19, workers were found to turn to mentors for role modeling, with women even more likely to do so (van Esch, Luse, & Bonner, 2021). Leaders need to show appropriate behaviors and reactions during a crisis. Both of these factors make the crisis seem more predictable and understandable.

Leaders in crisis also need to support their subordinates. This can be helping them to calm down and focus on what they themselves accomplish or do (Lacerda, 2019). It can also involve reducing the amount of threat felt by the crisis. While one leader cannot stop a crisis or its negative effects, a leader can make a person feel like they will still have a job in the future and will get support as needed. Thus, the leader is the superhero who helps reduce stress rather than the villain who creates it.

## Summary

People can't just be good leaders in times when everything is going well. All leaders will need to deal with stress felt for themselves and stress felt by their subordinates. And in times of crisis, this stress can be so big that it feels like you need superhuman strength to get through it. We may not have superhuman strength that makes us impervious to stress (which would be nice!), but by understanding stress and how to manage it, we can deal with it better for ourselves and those we work with.

Stress is a reaction to unpredictable and/or uncontrollable things in our environment (stressors) that we perceive to threaten us. Some stress can be good, but prolonged high stress has negative physical and psychological outcomes. As leaders, we need to avoid such high stress and protect our subordinates from it.

There are a number of ways to reduce stress. The best types of strategies are enactive strategies, where we change an environment to remove the stressor. These can take a lot of time and effort, like we saw with Banner and Hulk getting integrated, but the results can be incredible in reducing stress. Proactive strategies help too, where we learn skills that help us to generally deal with stress. Reactive strategies should be a last resort, but for an unexpected stressor, we may need to pull that all-nighter to get something done. A good leader focuses on enactive and proactive strategies.

When we are leaders in high stress and crisis situations, we need to work as best we can to reduce the stress of subordinates. This means making the situation feel less unpredictable and less threatening. Leaders need to be role models that others can look to for what to do. We need to be a shining example of the right thing to do as we often see Captain America be (and will talk about in a future chapter!).

Stress is something we all need to deal with, and a superhero leader will be someone who battles to reduce stress for themselves and those around them.

Chapter 7

# I Am Iron Man: Leader Authenticity, Self-awareness and Growth in Marvel Films

At the start of the first *Iron Man* movie, we would think that Tony Stark has a great life. He is rich, has won major awards, and is fawned over by attractive women. He seems to be able to just do whatever he wants. But, even as we are introduced to this, Stark himself seems bored, going through the motions. Is this really the life he wants?

This question becomes even more acute when he is kidnapped. He sees the weapons his company makes (and that have made him rich) be used to kill his own countrymen. In captivity, he sees his life as empty with no real personal relationships. He gets an injury to his heart that will likely affect him the rest of his life and could kill him. Stark leaves captivity feeling that his life needs to change, this life is not who he is or who he wants to be. This trajectory will lead him to become Iron Man, stop his company from profiting from war, and ultimately give his life for the good of the world.

This chapter will discuss Tony Stark as it relates to a person having self-awareness of who they really are and who they want to be, acting on that awareness by being authentic, and finally how aspects of being authentic can be beneficial for leaders as shown in the theory of authentic leadership. We will also discuss how you could be more self-aware and be the authentic person and leader your people need.

## Knowing the Hero You are

Self-awareness can be seen as people understanding their own personalities, characteristics, and what is important to them. We need to know not only our strengths but also our weaknesses and preferences. People cannot improve without having an accurate picture of themselves (Whetten & Cameron, 2020). People can have blind spots about themselves that lead them to make wrong choices and not work to improve where they may be deficient.

Early in *Iron Man* we see Tony Stark potentially lacking self-awareness. While he seems to be living the life of a rich playboy, he doesn't seem to have much enjoyment of it. This only becomes more true after his escape from captivity.

Leaders Assemble! Leadership in the MCU, 45–50
Copyright © 2022 by Gordon B. Schmidt and Sy Islam
Published under exclusive license by Emerald Publishing Limited
doi:10.1108/978-1-80117-670-520221007

He goes through the motions of his old life at times but increasingly devotes his time toward his Iron Man project. He becomes self-aware related to his company's behaviors related to selling weapons, as he now sees them as wrong and begins to work to change the company focus to one that he can feel proud of.

One reason that self-awareness can be difficult is that people often try to avoid criticism, especially when that criticism relates to something they see as an important part of themselves. People have what is called the "sensitive line," which is the point where a person becomes defensive when information threatens their self-concept (Whetten & Cameron, 2020). So if you see yourself as someone who is good at math, information that suggests you have a weakness related to math skills will often be resisted and negatively reacted to. On the other hand, if playing badminton is not important to your self-concept, information suggesting you lack skills at the game is unlikely to cause any distress. So this defensiveness only happens for areas important to you.

When people feel threatened or encounter uncomfortable information like this, they often have a threat-rigidity response (De Dreu & Nijstad, 2008). This response leads them to be more rigid in their behavior and thinking, looking to protect themselves and avoid risk. They cling to the familiar and comfortable in their thoughts and actions. This can mean the threatening information is ignored or discarded.

Tony Stark shows this in his reaction to times he needs the help of others. For changing his company and for finding a way to help heart condition, Tony is unwilling to ask for the help of others. His self-concept is focused on that he can accomplish anything – admitting he needs others – hits his sensitive line and threatens his self-concept. If he can't accomplish it on his own, it can't be done. This means he often struggles alone when others could help him. When he gets heart surgery in "Iron Man 3," he finally has accepted that he needs others to help him. This is important for his ability to lead in the future, although he still struggles with other challenges to his self-concept.

So if self-awareness is difficult to have but important, how can you develop and cultivate it? One important way is realizing that when you are defensive about something it might be a reaction to something that crosses your sensitive line. If you react more negatively to something another person suggests, it can be helpful to consider *why* you had such an extreme reaction. What does it say about your self-concept? Does the person have a point? Being reflective can help to gain insight from such happenings rather than reacting defensively and moving on.

Secondly, self-awareness is helped when we engage in self-disclosure with others and strengthen our relationships (Whetten & Cameron, 2020). When we have relationships with others where we share our own doubts and concerns, we are more likely to get honest feedback. This feedback can help us to see what we may be blind to and make needed changes. We can't self-disclose to everyone, but trusted relationships can be a good way to have an avenue to self-disclose our fears and to get the honest feedback we need to get. Tony Stark needs people like Pepper Potts and Captain America speaking truthfully to him, that is how he can grow as a person and improve.

## Being the Hero You are

When we have self-awareness, we can be more true to ourselves. Authenticity is when people act in line with their own core values, beliefs, personality, and motivation, creating alignment between a person's internal state and external expression of who they are (Harter, 2002). Authenticity has been found to benefit people in a number of ways, including higher life satisfaction, feeling connected to others, and a greater sense of personal meaning (Lehman, O'Connor, Kovacs, & Newman, 2019).

Despite the benefits of being authentic, we often are given advice to try to fit in or engage in impression management, outwardly showing what we believe others want us to be like. Gino, Sezer, and Huang (2020) call this catering, a tactic used where we intentionally try to behave in a way we think others will like, including going so far as to use verbal and nonverbal behavior we think fits with others' preferences.

While we might think this catering will help us, Gino et al. (2020) actually found the opposite for entrepreneurs pitching ideas to potential investors. Those who catered were given worse evaluations than those who were authentic. Those who were catering were found to be more anxious and felt more selfish, which may have in turn have hurt their performance. This catering takes its own energy and attention beyond what is needed to do the task normally.

Acting in a way different than who we are and how we feel can also have negative personal implications. Emotional labor is the idea that in a situation we express emotions that are different from how we actually feel, acting in a way we think is desired or appropriate for a situation. We are often asked in workplaces to display emotions other than what we really feel, especially in customer service interactions. Such displays of false emotions can have negative impacts on people, including greater feelings of stress, reduced job satisfaction, and reduced overall well-being (Lehman et al., 2019).

Thus, being authentic can help us to feel better and do better in our jobs, as while we may think pretending to feel or be a certain way helps us perform better the existing research doesn't support that idea. While we can't recommend just saying and doing whatever you want in your job, acting in a way more authentic to yourself is likely to make work better, both in terms of performance and your own well-being.

Tony Stark struggles with this authenticity in the Marvel Cinematic Universe (MCU) films. While we might see Tony as a brash individual who says and does what he wants, he does have an internal struggle in figuring out what he wants and how he should express himself. When in the first "Iron Man" he boldly declares that he is Iron Man (forgoing the tradition of a superhero secret identity), he is acting authentically in who he is – not someone to hide their identity behind the armor. He wants people to know that he is Tony Stark and that he is also Iron Man who saves the day. Tony is not a humble man and he wants to be that hero.

Where he struggles in future films is accepting this fact. He often talks about "quitting" being Iron Man and giving up the armor. He tries to do good in ways that don't involve him being out there front in center as Iron Man fighting bad guys. While such actions are laudable and might be authentic for other people, they don't represent who Tony is. Tony wants to be the one out there fighting the threat and feels a strong responsibility to others to be the person on that frontline saving the day. That is part of the reason why Tony always comes back to being Iron Man, even when it endangers and ultimately kills him. He feels the responsibility to be out there giving his all, even if he does find the idea of having a quiet life with his love Pepper Potts appealing. Tony's true and best self is being that hero defending the world.

In order to be a good leader, we too need to figure out what our authentic self is. How do we best make an impact? What is meaningful personally to us? When we try to deny our true selves we will not be the leader we could be. The idea of authentic leadership gets more directly at how authenticity can help us, particularly as a leader.

## Being the Leader You Can be

The idea of authentic leadership suggests that when a leader behaves in an authentic way, it has a positive impact on followers and performance. Authentic leaders foster self-awareness in themselves and others, are transparent in their relationships with followers, have a moral perspective, and ultimately create an environment for self-development (Walumbwa, Avolio, Gardner, Wernsing, & Peterson, 2008). Authentic leaders are leaders who show their "true self" to followers, not hiding their internal "true self" at work but presenting it openly. This honesty through authenticity is suggested to mean leaders act in ethical ways, although there is some controversy in the research literature as to if this always will be the case (Lehman et al., 2019). Perhaps it has most to do with what a person's "true self" is and the values that individual has that determine if their actions are seen as ethical by others.

The leader being authentic helps in many ways for the followers to be authentic, too. Authentic leadership is seen as providing a space for followers to become more personally self-aware, feel encouraged to be honest, and ultimately work to develop their own skills. Thus, the leader's authenticity is something that helps followers be authentic, helping to create a positive and productive work environment. And existing research finds many positive benefits for worker attitudes and performance when they are in such an environment (Lehman et al., 2019).

When examining the characteristics of authentic leadership, Bradley-Cole (2021) suggests two general categories, the leader being true to themselves and showing care and concern for others. Being true in this case relates to the leader showing consistency in their actions, being guided by an internal moral code. A follower doesn't need to agree with a leader every time but needs to feel that the leader has their own moral code and is not just doing what suits them in the moment. As we discussed before, an authentic person acts in accordance with their true self, not modifying their actions or beliefs based on what they think others might prefer. Thus, followers can expect consistency from the leader in their actions.

The second general category is care, that the authentic leader is someone who cares about their relationships with followers, acts with sincerity, and cares for the good of others. Followers believe an authentic leader will work to help them and are looking out for their needs. The leader will be sincere in working toward group goals and helping people obtain their own goals. An authentic leader advocates for the good of their followers and empowers them to act on their own as well. They may in fact put the good of their followers above their own personal needs due to the care they have for them.

Within the MCU films, we see Tony Stark exhibit a number of the characteristics of authentic leadership. While Tony may struggle with self-awareness and being authentic at times to himself, he often engages with others in an authentic way. Tony rarely holds back in expressing his true opinions and feelings. Other members of the Avengers can often see Tony express frustration and emotions in the moment. He is expressing how he truly feels. He is also willing to express his opinions on topics, and while others might not always agree (such as Captain America), people can accept they come from his own perspective of what needs to be done. Tony may think he is the smartest man in the room and be a wiseass, but he doesn't try to hide that nature that is an important part of him. The other Avengers always know where he stands and what he believes, whether they agree or not.

Tony Stark shows a great deal of care for the other members of the Avengers team. While he may be sarcastic in how he presents himself, he acts with sincerity in helping other team members and putting himself at risk time and time again for their benefit and the world's benefit. He is ultimately very dependable and can be counted on, even when the risk is great. Of all the Avengers in "Avengers: Endgame," he has the most to risk in returning to superheroics since he has a wife and daughter who need him. Despite not wanting to leave them, he ultimately needs to be true to himself – the hero Iron Man fighting on the frontline to save the world. His sacrifice shows the care he brings as an authentic leader.

While you may not have the extreme situations Tony Stark has to deal with in the MCU, you can engage in authentic leadership in your own life. To be an authentic leader, you need to first deepen your own self-awareness and get in touch with your own authentic self. Once you've done these things, being an authentic leader involves a few major things.

First, act in concert with your own authentic self in how you lead. You show your true self to others and show how your actions are driven by yourself. This allows followers to understand you and trust your behaviors and intention.

Second, show that you care about your relationships with followers and their well-being. When they feel this is the case, they will deepen their trust and want to perform well.

Third, cultivate authenticity in your followers. Help your followers to deepen their own self-awareness to discover their authentic self. Accept people when they are authentic, don't expect them to hide their emotions or who they are. If you tell them to be authentic and punish them for being so they will learn to hide their true selves.

Finally, support them in their own self-development. People will want to grow and develop their skills over time and authentic leaders help to cultivate such growth. Empower them with opportunities to make their own decisions and grow their own skills.

## Summary

To be our best as leaders, self-awareness and authenticity are crucial. Deepening our understanding of these concepts and applying them to ourselves helps us to be the best leader we can be. Watching the journey of Tony Stark helps show us the difficult but important path toward authenticity. The way may be hard, but it can lead to authentic leadership and the benefits it entails.

We began this chapter talking about how while Tony Stark at the start of "Iron Man" seemed to have it all but he was in fact dissatisfied. Self-awareness helps us to determine what we really value and who our true self is. For personal growth and improvement we need to understand who we are and thus see where we need and want to grow. Self-awareness is a crucial initial step for growth. And self-awareness can be hard! We often avoid criticism, especially if it seems to threaten something we think is important to us. This reflection and criticism is important for us to be self-aware, ultimately.

Being self-aware of who we are gives us the potential to live in authenticity – living in tune with our true self. Many times in life we may feel pressure or temptation to act not in concert with our true beliefs and feelings. Doing so can seem like the "right" or "easy" thing to do through catering or emotional labor. However, not being authentic relates negatively to personal well-being and can in fact result in actually performing worse. Being authentic can lead to positive results. Tony Stark struggles with trying to quit being Iron Man and often being miserable about it. That is a struggle because Tony is not being authentic – being a hero like Iron Man on the frontline helping to save others is an important part of his true self. We need to be authentic to our true selves, not just being what we think others want us to be.

When we are self-aware and authentic, we have the baseline we need to engage in authentic leadership. Authentic leadership involves leaders being true to themselves, helping others to be their authentic selves, and caring about their followers. Followers believe the leader is being truthful and cares about their well-being. Authentic leadership can lead to positive work environments and people performing at higher levels (Lehman et al., 2019).

This chapter helped us all consider how authenticity can have an important role in our success as a leader. We can all be authentic leaders in the groups we are a part of whether, big, small, or made up of superheroes. The first step is self-awareness and starting that journey to find our authentic self.

Chapter 8

# Should We Open Up Wakanda?
# Leader Roles in External Relations

One key question for the Black Panther is how Wakanda should deal with outside countries. Wakanda had shrouded itself in mystery, and other nations had
little knowledge of its resources and power. This is at the heart of the introduction of the Black Panther character. Wakanda and in turn the Black Panther has
enormous power and resources. The nation can lead, but they choose not to. The
decision to engage with external forces is an important one for any organization
and leader.

One of the core challenges of leadership is how a leader deals with other teams
and organizations. Many of the leadership theories that we have discussed in this
book have focused on how leaders can best lead their own teams and organizations. But we can't forget the important role that leaders play in modeling values
and the core purpose of an organization. Leaders serve an important decision-
making role in dealing with the world outside of their teams and organizations.
In this chapter, we'll discuss the ways in which leaders interact with external individuals, teams, and organizations. We'll look at how leaders' functions extend
beyond their responsibilities to members of their own team, to how they manage
and deal with the external environment. We will also focus on how leaders can
function effectively within a multiteam system. Whether you're a Wakandan or
not, as a leader you must interact and negotiate with other groups to improve the
position of your organization.

## Wakanda Isolated Forever?

Leaders make choices in how they deal with the external environment. The
external environment in which their organization functions has an impact on
all levels of the choices a leader might make. Mumford, Zaccaro, Harding,
Jacobs, and Fleishman (2000) proposed a leadership skills model comprised of
five components: (a) individual attributes, (b) competencies, (c) environmental
influences, (d) career experiences, and (d) leadership outcomes. This model
posits that career experiences along with individual attributes (personality and

Leaders Assemble! Leadership in the MCU, 51–57
Copyright © 2022 by Gordon B. Schmidt and Sy Islam
Published under exclusive license by Emerald Publishing Limited
doi:10.1108/978-1-80117-670-520221008

cognitive ability), and competencies (i.e., problem solving and social skills) lead to leadership outcomes like problem-solving and team performance. A leader's skill development, career development, and personal development are all impacted by external influences. External influences to the leader may be internal or external to the organization itself. Internal influences include follower skills and available technology. External influences may include political, social, and economic issues. These factors all affect a leader's skill development over time. While the Mumford et al. (2000) model does not prescribe specific external factors, it does acknowledge that these factors exist and impact leader behavior and development.

Leaders are impacted by the outside world in terms of opportunity and challenges. Their living environments, educational opportunities, and career experiences impact their ability to develop the skills and experiences necessary to run an organization. The external environment is one in which the leader is consistently negotiating and working within.

Wakanda's relationship with the outside world has been a fraught one. One of the first things we learn about Wakanda is its isolationist position. When the nation is introduced in Captain America: Civil War, no one believes the country has much to offer since it's viewed as a backward nation with little technology. Wakandan isolation is a response to the outside world. Wakandan leaders saw the world around them and made a strategic choice. Rather than seek support from the world, or try to engage the world in world affairs, the Wakandan leaders decide to keep to themselves. Even among the Wakandans, there is a tribe (the Jabari) that chooses not to engage even with Wakanda. Thus, we see isolation upon isolation. This choice of leaders of the past is the central conflict in Black Panther. The experience of Wakandan leaders with the outside world has made them wary of dealings with outsiders. Given the vast mineral resources of Wakanda, they have opted to focus on developing their own internal technology by using their vast resource of vibranium.

Using our Mumford et al.'s (2000) leadership skills model, we can see why this choice was repeated so often by Wakandan leaders. Each leader of Wakanda grew up in Wakanda, their education was within Wakanda, and they developed Wakandan leadership competencies. Their environment was primarily Wakanda with little experience of the outside world. Or as Prince N'Jobu and Nakia did they only engaged in the outside world as spies. By going out into the world with a hidden agenda, Wakandan leaders consistently see the world outside of Wakanda through the lens of isolation. Thus, the development process of leaders for Wakanda reinforces their view the external world is to be avoided rather than supported. We start to see a change in this leadership thought process with T'Challa. T'Challa has a complex experience with Captain America, Iron Man, and Baron Zemo after the death of his father. T'Challa fights alongside the Avengers and learns the value of their camaraderie, going so far as to help the man he believed had murdered his father, Bucky Barnes, the Winter Soldier. Unlike many previous leaders of Wakanda, T'Challa interacts with the world by fully engaging with the Avengers and the dangers they face. His career experiences are vastly different from other Wakandan leaders, and these experiences inform his actions in later films. T'Challa's Wakandan upbringing helps to differentiate him from Captain

America and Iron Man during their battle against Baron Zemo. T'Challa learns that pursuing vengeance above all else is not a healthy approach to resolving his conflict against Zemo, and unlike Iron and Captain America, T'Challa is able to let his anger go to pursue justice.

We can contrast the lessons that T'Challa learned with those of his cousin Erik Killmonger. Killmonger's experiences growing up amid the racism of the United States and fighting in its wars taught him a strong mistrust of the outside world. When Killmonger sees the power of Wakanda, he sees only the power to dominate. Unlike Wakandan leaders who look to conserve their power within the boundaries of Wakanda, Killmonger sees a powerful force for domination and revenge. Killmonger's experiences in the outside world have corrupted his worldview, and as a leader, he is able to use his considerable skills to bring like-minded people along. When he interacted with W'Kabi, Killmonger persuaded this Wakandan chief that only he can bring about justice for Wakanda through domination. Thus, the leadership skills that Killmonger has gained are turned toward the outside world but not to work in collaboration, only domination. He takes the lessons he learned from war and covert operations and brings them to Wakanda, a place that can provide him the resources for his villainous goals.

A major reason for Wakandan hesitancy in engaging with the world at large has to do with their vibranium resources. Vibranium is a unique element that powers Wakanda's technology and provided the necessary environmental changes for the Black Panther to gain their strength and enhanced senses. Roth (1995) posits that some leaders view the world from a resource-based perspective and that can impact their leadership style and impact on a firm. In the resource-based model, the argument is made that organizations are unique bundles of resource stocks and that leaders make choices that affect the amount of resource stocks that exist in these organizations. Essentially, CEOs can view their organization as a finite set of resources that must be managed, shared, and replenished. This approach is an important one to consider when thinking of Wakandan leaders' decision-making. All aspects of Wakandan life are meant to be kept under control so that the nation can protect its primary resource: vibranium. The artifice that the nation maintains is to protect its people and the source of their competitive advantage. Even altruistic actions such as Nakia's spy mission are tempered by the need for Wakanda to hide its power. Upon saving a group of refugees with T'Challa and Nakia, Okoye cautions the refugees to speak to no one of what they saw. The secrecy is of utmost importance to maintaining the nation's strategic competitive advantage.

While maintaining secrecy for a team or for a leader is important, it can raise serious issues. The lack of knowledge that the outside world has about Wakanda leads to issues when T'Challa deals with Everett Ross, his US liaison. Without any clear information about Wakanda, T'Challa cannot deal with Ross on an equal footing. They have little trust until Ross sees Wakanda for himself and T'Challa is able to bring him to his way of thinking about what's best for the nation.

As a leader, maintaining some secrecy may be of importance to protect your organization. But too much secrecy may breed distrust among potential allies. It's up to a leader to scan the environment and identify potential partners as well as eschew potential threats. This delicate balancing act is what T'Challa tries to achieve as king of Wakanda. While you may not be leading an organization with the type of resources of Wakanda, it is still important to identify what information to share and how best to present yourself to fellow teams and organizational leaders.

## Relationship Building as Nation Building

In Chapter 3, we discussed the importance of team leadership using the Hill model of leadership (Zaccaro et al., 2001). Leaders must not only deal with their teams internally but must also consider their actions as symbols externally as well. This is especially important when engaging in external negotiations or dealing with external factors. In addition to the internal team behaviors that a leader must use to maintain their team, the Hill model also posits environmental behaviors such as networking, advocating, negotiating, and sharing information. These behaviors are especially important for teams within organizations and those teams that deal across organizations.

The Hill model applies the McGrath's critical leadership functions or functional leadership. Functional leadership defines a leader's behavior as being focused on within the team (internal actions) or out of the team (external actions) that follow either a monitoring or executive action approach (McGrath as cited in Northouse, 2022). Monitoring is observing or diagnosing a problem. Executive action is the attempt to solve the problem that the leader chooses. Carter et al. (2020) expand this model to an interteam context. These researchers propose that leaders can look at actions to take across systems or team outcomes. Systems represent a group of teams (or in some cases of organizations) and team outcomes represent the output of specific teams (either functional within an organization or a group of organizations). This may seem like a complex approach to team building, but we have seen this approach used often in the Marvel Cinematic Universe. For example, when facing Ronan the Accuser, the Guardians of the Galaxy use a multiteam system involving the Ravager Army, the Nova Corps, and the Guardians themselves. This is a complex system where the team's leadership can choose to focus on one of the multiple subteams or provide instructions across all the teams (system).

As a leader, it may be beneficial to view yourself and your team as a part of a multiteam system where you interact with other teams inside of your organization. For example, if you work in information technology (IT) in your organization, you provide support to other teams like sales. Sales interact with those outside of your organization and along with the IT department forms a system in which customer and provider work together systemically.

Leaders who can see themselves as a part of a system and can make decisions that impact these systems effectively are crucial to the future of leadership. As a leader, you not only have to manage your team but your customers and other important stakeholders. Effective leaders are systems thinkers and never focus solely on their own team to the exclusion of monitoring the external environment.

## The Conquerors or the Conquered

Leaders who deal with external teams or customer groups have a few options in how they may approach those outside of their organizations. The Hill model of leadership (Zaccaro et al., 2001) offers a few behaviors that may be of value to leaders of external facing teams. The first is networking and forming alliances. Strong leaders build relationships that serve both their organization and others. These alliances are built on relationships between leaders and an agreement that their teams and organizations will support one another during their engagement. T'Challa intimately understands the value of building relationships. When he battles M'Baku at the waterfall, he could treat M'Baku as the conquered and kill him. Instead, he asks that M'Baku yield because his people need him. This action builds an unspoken alliance between these two leaders that bears fruit when it's time to retake Wakanda from Killmonger. M'Baku saves T'Challa's life in return.

The relationship between M'Baku and T'Challa allows T'Challa to engage in another important external leader behavior. T'Challa can negotiate upward. Not only does he get M'Baku's support in healing him, but he convinces M'Baku to provide his army in the battle against Killmonger and the Wakandan forces. T'Challa's ethical clarity and advocacy allow him to reach across generations of conflict to build a strong relationship.

Another important action for leaders when dealing with external organizations is advocating and representing the team to the external world. This is a key element to Wakanda's position. Wakanda's chosen position in hiding itself from the world has its own drawbacks. During their interactions, Okoye and T'Challa are often subtly disrespected by others, especially Agent Ross, who believes that Wakanda and its leadership have little to offer. It is only after Ross experiences the technological might of Wakanda that he becomes an effective ally. The perspective of outsiders is also important in how T'Challa acts in the Black Panther costume is symbolic of Wakanda. This is the reason that T'Challa chooses not to kill Klaw in South Korea. There are too many people watching him potentially perform an execution. If Wakanda wishes to enter the world stage, a murderous king will not be received well. T'Challa must advocate in different ways.

For T'Challa to advocate for Wakanda effectively and to negotiate more powerful relationships with external allies, he must repudiate Wakanda's isolationism. When T'Challa confronts his father in the afterlife, he highlights this lack of moral clarity in Wakanda's actions. Wakandan leadership has consistently eschewed following through on their ethical obligations. Ethical leadership theory states that ethical leaders should be honest and principled decision makers (Brown & Treviño, 2006). Since King T'Chaka's actions are so objectionable, moral clarity is needed for T'Challa to bring Wakanda's values to the outside world.

Even though T'Challa has greater moral clarity than his father, this moral clarity is hard won. When he has the opportunity to explain who Killmonger is to the council, T'Challa hesitates and attempts to remove Killmonger from the chamber. T'Challa can only become a king worthy of leading Wakanda to the outside world when he reveals that Killmonger is royalty and accepts his challenge. T'Challa must show that he can engage in another important external leadership behavior, which is sharing all information with his team. They need the knowledge for their nation to engage with others on the world stage.

We can contrast T'Challa's commitment to the truth with his father T'Chaka's choice to treat the existence of his nephew N'Jadaka as information that his team must be protected from. Effective team leaders must make sound decisions about what team members must be protected from, but this was an incorrect choice on the part of T'Chaka. T'Challa keeps his team informed and often this information provides the resources that his team needs to perform effectively.

T'Challa and Killmonger differ most greatly in their view of Wakandan effectiveness. Both men agree that Wakanda should do more, but they differ in approach. Killmonger orders his team using coercive action to build weapons and share them with the rest of the world. Killmonger sees Wakanda as a conqueror, going so far as to convince W'Kabi that there can only be conquerors or the conquered. T'Challa views the world with a more open, less binary perspective. He sees partnerships where Killmonger only sees enemies. Killmonger even views those in Wakanda as enemies, his actions are virtually all task focused at the expense of relationships. When T'Challa returns, the Dora Milaje immediately turn on Killmonger because he has been so focused on external enemies that he has not maintained any relationships. Killmonger solidified this view when he burned the sacred heart-shaped herb, even future kings are potential enemies to Killmonger.

T'Challa chooses to reach out to the world once he solidifies his position as king. He follows Nakia's plan to begin to build scientific outreach to the world. These efforts bring more allies to Wakanda. These relationships become especially important when the Avengers face Thanos. Wakanda, a place that had been closed off for so long becomes the site of the final battle against Thanos on Earth, where the Avengers battle until the "snap." During this battle, the importance of coordination among multiteam systems becomes apparent as teams of heroes face off against Thanos' minions. The Wakandan guard, the Jabari army, and a variety of Avengers battle to protect the Vision and his Infinity Stone. Each team has a clear mandate and knows exactly what they must do as they face Thanos. Despite not being able to defeat Thanos (the time stone provides many opportunities, just ask Dr Strange!), the team's function effectively. Each team shared information with a variety of team members, so they could step up at different times as needed.

The openness of Wakanda to be the battleground against Thanos is an enormous change that has been brought about by T'Challa's leadership. His ability to maintain strong relationships even with those who may oppose him and his ability to convince disparate groups of people to work together for their own best interests. As a team leader, when dealing with external stakeholders, you need to consider how best to manage the situation. Monitor the situation for your team and make the decisions that best suit your situation. As the example of Killmonger shows, treating negotiations as a zero-sum game won't always work out in your best interest. Building relationships, communicating effectively, and staying focused on the needs of your team as well as team effectiveness will bear the most fruit.

As a leader, understanding how to build effective relationships both within your team and outside of your team can help your become a better leader. By understanding the external environment, the needs of your team/organization, and how best to leverage relationships, you can learn to lead your team into a new world.

## Summary

In this chapter, we focused on how leaders managed external relationships for their teams and organizations. We started by talking about a leadership skills model that included the components: (a) individual attributes, (b) competencies, (c) environmental influences, (d) career experiences, and (e) leadership outcomes. Each component was affected by the external environment. A leader comes into a leadership after being affected by the external environment and their perspective on how best to deal with external stakeholders and organizations can be understood by understanding those external factors.

We also discussed the Hill model of team leadership and focused on the external factors that a leader must consider as a team leader. Effective team leaders assess the external environment, network with those outside of their team, advocate for their team, protect their team members from the outside environment, share relevant information with team members, and negotiate for better positions for their teams and organizations. Leaders must consider all of these factors especially as they function in complex multiteam systems with a variety of stakeholders.

# Chapter 9

# Am I a Hero, an X-men, a Mutant, or Just a Menace? Leadership and Identity

Throughout the X-men films, we see multiple leaders trying to define what it means to be a mutant, a person born with special powers due to their genetics. Professor Xavier wants mutants to see themselves as heroes, protectors of all people, and members of the human race. Magneto wants mutants to see themselves as separate from humanity, as a next step in evolution that needs to defend itself from the prejudices of normal humans. Meanwhile, nonmutant leaders in the film define mutants as other, as not human, as menaces to humanity that need to be controlled or that being a mutant as a disease that needs to be "cured."

Leaders will often play a crucial role in how followers see themselves and their identity. In this chapter, we will talk about how leaders can engage in sensemaking, helping followers to interpret what is happening and how they fit in an organization or groups. We will look at the concept of organizational identification, the groups a person feels connected to, and what the person sees as the elements of that identity. This identification can help them to be more committed to the organization. Finally, we'll talk about how you can apply this to your own team of heroes, mutants, or even just normal employees!

## Making Sense of Mutants

Sensemaking is a process we see in all groups and organizations, as people try to interpret events, people, and ideas in the world around them (Maitlis & Christianson, 2014). Things that result in a greater need for sensemaking will be those that seem potentially relevant to the person but that are seen as confusing and/ or different from what is expected. So if a company fires its CEO, unexpectedly workers at the company are likely to want to make sense of the situation and how it affects them. In the film "X-men: Last Stand," a "cure" for being a mutant is developed and those who are mutants need to make sense of what this means for mutants, if is it a good thing, and of course if the "cure" is something they should consider for themselves. The interpretation of the event will then drive a person's opinions and action, whether it be supporting a new CEO or trying to destroy the new mutant "cure."

Leaders Assemble! Leadership in the MCU, 59–64

Copyright © 2022 by Gordon B. Schmidt and Sy Islam

Published under exclusive license by Emerald Publishing Limited

doi:10.1108/978-1-80117-670-520221009

While people individually engage in sensemaking (think about your own experiences making sense of an unexpected event!), leaders will often play a crucial role in making sense of events for their followers. Leaders will help to define what events are meaningful for followers and how they should react and feel toward them (Smircich & Morgan, 1982). The leader provides a frame for the followers to understand what has happened and how it fits with previously held values and goals. They may also help to frame feelings and emotions a person should feel related to the event (Mikkelsen & Wahlin, 2020). All of this impacts the follower's future actions.

Within the X-men films, we see multiple leaders try to influence how a mutant should be seen and what mutants should do. People having these powers are "unexpected" and thus people look to leaders to define what mutants are. This is true for both people who are mutants and those in the general public who do not have mutant powers.

Professor Charles Xavier offers a vision of mutants as part of humanity whose powers allow them to help others as heroes. He runs "Xavier's School for Gifted Youngsters," a place where adolescents are trained in safe use of their powers and some students graduate to being members of the X-men, a team of mutants devoted to superheroics. Note here that he has framed this as a school. This is not a prison for mutants or a military base, or even a refuge, it is a place of learning. The people who attend the school are also classified as "gifted," their mutant powers are a good thing, something that allows them to help others. Mutants who attend Xavier's school or even just know about it can feel that they are gifted people that can give back to the world. We could see this as sensemaking that mutants are gifted humans that can be trained to have a positive impact on the world for all. Mutants are not to be feared by nonmutants and mutants should focus on how they can help humanity as a whole.

This sensemaking of Xavier's suggests the possibility of peaceful coexistence between mutants and the non-powered rest of humanity. This framing, however, is unfortunately not held by everyone, with other mutants and nonmutants alike framing mutants differently. These leaders have different goals and opinions, which shape how they make sense of mutants and their role in the world.

Magneto offers a very different sensemaking than Xavier. Magneto sees mutants as the next step in evolution. Mutants are not humans, they are the next step and thus will dominate the future. Normal humans are framed as a threat to mutants. Magneto argues to his followers that humans fear what they don't understand and that they will act on this fear by killing mutants or taking away their powers. Magneto's framing of normal humans as a threat draws on his own experiences as a Jew in a concentration camp during World War II. He has seen how horrific people can treat those they see as different. As such, Magneto puts protecting fellow mutants as more important than helping nonmutants or the world at large. He sees mutants and nonmutants as on opposite sides of a war. Thus, in the sensemaking of Magneto, mutants need to see themselves as different from nonmutants and protect themselves from current and future threats from normal humans. Mutants need to band together.

Nonmutant leaders in the films also engage in sensemaking related to mutants. Generally, they are engaging in sensemaking for how nonmutants should see mutants and react to them. One common frame placed on mutants by such leaders is that mutants are dangerous to humans and should not be seen as humans themselves. In the first "X-men" film, US Senator Robert Kelly leads a campaign that mutants be required to register with the government. Senator Kelly frames this as reasonable due to the fact that mutants are dangerous like weapons due to their powers. Mutants are dangers, not people.

We also see nonmutant leaders frame mutants as a disease. Warren Worthington II and his Worthington Labs create a "cure" for mutants that is supposed to remove their powers permanently. For Worthington, mutants are afflicted with mutant powers in a similar way to a disease or mental illness. Mutants are a danger to not just others but to themselves. The "cure" removes the problem of being a mutant. Thus, normal humans should feel sorry for mutants but now that there is a cure, they can be "fixed" and go back to being normal humans. This perspective makes sense of mutants as a disease to be cured, not something to be valued or embraced.

As you can see, all of these leaders are reacting to the same events, the existence of mutants, but each is engaging in different sensemaking that suggests a different understanding of mutants and what should be done about them. As a leader, we are often called to make judgments of what is important and how our organization should respond. If our major competitor announces layoffs, is that good news for us (we must be doing a "better" job) or a bad sign (people don't care about our products as much as they used to)? When you engage in leadership, you will often be asked to make such a call and to convince others to see things your way. Doing so will help your team to be on the same page and act in concert with each other, rather than each person doing their own sensemaking and perhaps working at cross purposes. When sensemaking is done well, the people on your team also feel well connected with each other. We will talk about one aspect of feeling connected next, which is organizational identification.

## "I'm an X-Men Now!" Identification with an Organization or Team

Organizational identification is the degree to which people define themselves based on an organization or group they are part of. Those who identify strongly with their organization are very beneficial to that organization as they tend to be more motivated, loyal, and actually perform better (Blader, Patil, & Parker, 2017). This identification can be based on a number of things, but organization-relevant events and the sensemaking an organization makes around them can have a significant impact. This can be especially true during major crises such as COVID-19, where organizations need to make painful choices that show what an organization truly values and finds important (Ashforth, 2020). Can the organization make sense of a situation in a way that keeps people feeling connected to the organization or will it ring false to employees and hurt identification?

We certainly see aspects of organization identification in the X-men films. A number of mutants feel a strong tie to Xavier's school and the X-men team. To the members of the X-men, the team and school are something they are willing to lay down their lives for if needed. When Wolverine first gets involved with the X-men, he is distrustful of Xavier and the team, but over time, he begins to strongly identify with the team, going so far as to risk his own life traveling through time in "X-men: Days of Future Past." This shows his strong motivation and his identification with Xavier's dream of humans and mutants working together. Wolverine finds in the X-men a group that helps him to feel he belongs and matters, an affiliation motive common in organizational identification (Ashforth, 2016). We also see the X-men wear matching costumes, again showing a focus on the organization itself (the X-men) rather than their own individual interests.

Magneto also offers the potential for strong identification from mutants that join up with his cause. Magneto creates the "Brotherhood of Mutants," an organization exclusively for mutants who work together to protect themselves from normal humans and create a place for mutants to live together. He suggests that mutants shouldn't identify with humans but should instead see themselves as above humans and be able to be themselves as nature intended. This could be a very appealing argument to some mutants and we see the young mutant Pyro leave the X-men to join this brotherhood. This brotherhood offers an identity for mutants who feel disconnected from normal humans.

Leaders across organizations will often want to build the connectedness seen in organizational identification. Think about your experiences in organizations where leaders have tried to make you feel like part of the organization and proud of what the organization does. This can be leaders of the whole organization, like a CEO, but it can also be leaders of a particular team or work group. When your team identifies with the team and sees it as a meaningful part of who they are, you will have a team that can do incredible things, as we see with a team like the X-men. People who feel connected will in turn often feel a strong commitment to the group or organization, which we will talk about in the next section.

## "I'm an X-Men for Life!" Commitment to an Organization or Team

Organizational commitment is the desire of a person to remain part of the organization and to work toward its goals. People who are committed are more likely to stay, are more motivated, miss less work, and perform better (Yahaya & Ebrahim, 2016). The sensemaking and identification we have talked about earlier in this chapter can both make workers feel more committed to their organization.

Research has found three general components of commitment, and we can see all three within the X-men films. These types of commitment all impact the actions that a character takes.

The first component is called affective commitment and is the degree that a person feels a strong emotional commitment to an organization and wants to stay a part of it (Meyer & Allen, 1991). So those with high affective commitment often have strong identification with the organization and its values. So we can see that commitment with many of the X-men, who believe in Xavier's mission and will work hard to make it succeed. On the low end of affective commitment, we could see a character like Pyro, who didn't feel that much emotional connection with the X-men's mission of working with humanity and thus left to join the Brotherhood of Mutants instead. The brotherhood had a mission that fit better with his own desires.

The second component of commitment is called continuance commitment and is the degree a person feels they don't have other options of something to be a part of that has the same benefits (Meyer & Allen, 1991). In many cases, this can be people with specialized skills or experiences that give them high pay or status in one organization but that wouldn't transfer to other organizations. This was seen in the United States with some autoworkers who had good pay and status in their current plant but who had trouble finding jobs when the plant closed down. The best place for their pay and status was that plant due to their plant-specific skills. We certainly might think some mutants stay with the X-men or brotherhood because they don't have good options elsewhere. In such a case, it is less about believing in the organization's mission as not having good options. If an option arises, they may leave. We see that in part in "X-men: Last Stand," as Rogue is willing to consider taking the mutant "cure" rather than remain a mutant. Her powers hurt her ability to connect with others and the X-men is one of the few places she can feel connected. However, if her powers can be removed, she would not have the same need and could go back to living a "normal" life.

The third component of commitment is called normative commitment and is the degree a person feels an obligation to feel connected and part of the organization (Meyer & Allen, 1991). So if you feel like your organization gave you your "big break" or supported you during an important time you might feel like you should support it in return. For Wolverine, the help the X-men have given him related to finding out his past could lead to a feeling of obligation to stay with the X-men. Meanwhile, Xavier felt that Mystique owes him and the X-men and thus should have stayed an X-men rather than teaming up with Magneto. In this example, Xavier feels like Mystique should feel normative commitment and thus stay loyal to the X-men. She doesn't feel that loyalty and thus is willing to leave the X-men. This is an important aspect of normative commitment – it is what the person perceives. Others might feel you "owe" your organization loyalty, but for normative commitment, it matters only how you personally feel.

So a person's overall commitment to an organization is made up of these three components. Leaders can help to increase these levels of commitment in their followers. So when Magneto or Xavier talks about the mission of their respective organizations they may be helping a follower to identify more with the organization and deepen their emotional connection with the organization (affective commitment). When members of Magneto's Brotherhood of Mutants do illegal actions, it becomes harder for them to go back to a normal life, which might make them feel more like they have nowhere else to go (continuance commitment). When Xavier helps a mutant to better control their powers and provides them a safe place to live, he is potentially increasing their feelings of obligation to stay part of the X-men (normative commitment). While there can be ethical concerns with how you increase commitment (such as Magneto and illegal actions), good leaders will generally be increasing the commitment of their followers over time and gaining the benefits of a more committed workforce.

## Summary

Leaders can have a big impact on how followers see the world and their place in it. In this chapter, we discussed this in a few ways, looking to the X-men films as sources of examples and lessons. Leaders help followers to make sense of what is going in the world. Leaders also impact how much a follower identifies with an organization or group, seeing its interests as the follower's own. Finally, we looked at the different ways a person can feel commitment to an organization or group and how leaders play a role in this.

Those engaging in leadership will often need to interpret the world for their followers. When the unexpected or confusing happens, this sensemaking is especially important. Leaders will help the whole team to get on the same page, seeing an event in the same way and doing appropriate actions for that perspective. While the X-men films are full of unexpected events that make them engaging entertainment, in the real world, we also have to deal with the unexpected. A good leader is able to frame an event in a way that makes sense to followers and fits with the goals and values of an organization.

People often want to feel like they belong, and organizational identification helps us to think about how people can feel a strong connection to an organization and its goals. This identification makes the goals of their organization their own goals, driving action and greater motivation. Both Xavier and Magneto offer strong visions that their followers can identify with and make part of their own self-definition. A good leader will help a follower to understand what an organization is about and how it can fit with the personal identity of the follower.

Finally, we talked about the three components of organizational commitment (affective, continuance, normative). Each of these components impacts how committed a person is to their organization, wanting to remain in the organization and work toward its goals. Each component has a different reason for being commitment, and thus people might differ widely across the dimension. Leaders can help people to feel more committed to the organization through their own actions such as presenting the importance of organization goals, making people feel the organization is the best place for them, and helping followers in ways that build their loyalty to the organization.

Leaders need to think carefully about how they help followers to make sense of the world and how followers see the organization and what it does for them. Leaders can't just assume everyone is on the same page. This chapter gives you some advice and things to consider as you help create meaning, influence attitudes, and motivate actions of your own followers now and in the future.

Chapter 10

# Everything Begins with a (Her)o

While across the Marvel films we see leaders vary in a number of different ways, one way we don't see nearly enough variety is gender. Leaders in Marvel films, both officially designated and otherwise, are predominantly male. Female leaders are rare and gender nonconforming or transgender leaders are nonexistent.

In this chapter, we will discuss this lack of women in leadership roles is unfortunately present in our real life world as well. We will discuss some of the reasons this takes place, such as implicit theories, even though research evidence suggests that men and women perform at similar levels in leadership roles (Gipson, Pfaff, Mendelsohn, Catenacci, & Burke, 2017). We will explore how women are often given leadership opportunities in times of crisis or bad performance (such as Black Widow during the five-year gap period). We will then highlight how we as leaders can help make our organizations a more welcoming and supportive place for female leaders, making sure we have the (her)oes we need to be successful.

## A Lack of (Her)oes

While women make up about half the US workforce, they are not nearly as represented in major leadership roles (Gipson et al., 2017). For companies in the Fortune 500, only about 8% have a female CEO and only 1% (2 people) are Black women (Hinchcliffe, 2021). Looking globally, only 31% of senior leadership roles in businesses are held by women (Grant Thornton, 2021). Women are underrepresented across leadership roles in the world, an idea often described as a "glass ceiling," where female or minority group members are unable to attain leadership positions beyond certain lower level positions.

There are a number of reasons that this is the case. Gender stereotypes and discrimination of course are a major cause of this, as these impact women across work settings (Gipson et al., 2017). This issue can be compounded, however, as leadership roles have their own set of beliefs people have about what a leader is and should be "like."

Implicit theories are beliefs, often relatively unconscious, that people have about the world and how things work. In the case of leaders, these beliefs are about who should be a leader and what makes an effective leader. One major aspect found in implicit leadership theories is that men and masculine traits are

**Leaders Assemble! Leadership in the MCU, 65–70**
**Copyright © 2022 by Gordon B. Schmidt and Sy Islam**
**Published under exclusive license by Emerald Publishing Limited**
**doi:10.1108/978-1-80117-670-520221010**

seen as appropriate for leadership roles, an idea that has been called "think leader, think male." Research by Koenig, Eagly, Mitchell, and Ristikari (2011) looked at a number of different studies in a meta-analysis and found that indeed culturally masculine traits and male stereotypes are perceived more strongly similar to leadership traits and effectiveness.

When considering what a leader should be like, people often focus on agentic characteristics, the idea that a person is individualistic, confident, and assertive. These characteristics are more often associated with male stereotypes, with female stereotypes focused more on women being warm and communal focused (Gipson et al., 2017). Relatedly, people who show the trait of dominance in terms of being confident, forceful, and persuasive are more likely to be perceived to be a leader and effective as a leader. This personality trait fits with more masculine stereotypes, and research suggests that it relates positively to leadership perceptions only for men, not women. Women who are more dominant are not perceived as better leaders and in fact can be seen negatively as a leader due to not fitting existing gender stereotypes for women (Kim et al., 2020).

That masculinity is associated strongly with implicit theories of what leaders are like is detrimental to women aspiring to be leaders, as they are less likely to be seen as a good "fit" for leadership roles. People in an ambiguous situation are more likely to think a man is the leader versus a woman, although that effect is lessened when the person making the judgment is female (Jackson, Engstrom, & Emmers-Sommer, 2007).

These implicit values and concerns of discrimination are also likely to play a role in the fact women are generally less likely to aspire to leadership roles. Research by Hoyland et al. (2021) found that in a sample of 18- to 20-year-olds, the degree a person was confident they could be effective as a leader (leader self-efficacy) related more strongly to a motivation to lead in their career for men than women. So men who felt they could be effective as a leader were more motivated to be a leader in their career. Women were less influenced to want to be a leader in their career, even though they felt they had the ability to be one. In a study by Goodwin, Dodson, Chen, and Diekmann (2020),when asked to consider joining an online leadership committee that was majority-male, women compared to men felt they would have less power in the committee and had less intentions to try to join the committee. Thus, we might think women who could be capable as leaders may not step up and seek out leadership roles as they feel unlikely to be chosen or given power even if in a leadership role.

Within the Marvel Cinematic Universe (MCU) and Marvel films, we unfortunately see these issues of leadership roles filled predominately by male (and white) leaders. Characters like Captain America and Iron Man might be good leaders overall, but they do well fit with implicit theories of leaders having masculine qualities. Both can be seen as having a high level of being agentic and trait dominance, even if they may lead in different ways. A character like Captain Marvel with her military and Kree training might seem like someone well suited for a leadership role, but she does not get real opportunities to be a leader in the MCU, mostly working on her own (although within the comic books she has been a leader at times). Captain Marvel in fact is targeted by discrimination by her peers as to whether she "belongs" in the air force as a pilot (a male-dominated profession). Captain Marvel's Kree commander Yon-Rogg also acts like she needs to "prove herself" to him, although it is unclear if that is due to her gender or the fact she is from Earth. Captain Marvel could have stayed on Earth at the end of her film but instead goes to space on her own, making her own path. While that might be the right path for her personally, her leadership on Earth might have been hugely influential when other heroes began to appear in the MCU timeline.

## Why Don't You Fix it: The Lack of Good Opportunities for Female Leaders

While we have talked about the lack of female leaders in general, problems can result as well for what leadership opportunities women are actually offered. Women can be offered leadership roles in difficult situations where failure is likely. These situations don't set up women leaders for success as leaders and may mean their time of leadership opportunity is short.

Research has found that women are more likely to be selected for senior leadership roles in situations where an organization or group is in a state of crisis, risk, or high chance of failure, an idea that has been called the "glass cliff" (Gipson et al., 2017; Glass & Cook, 2016). While the glass ceiling suggests women can't rise above a certain level of leadership, the glass cliff suggests that women are put into leadership roles where things are or could go badly, hence the cliff the leader might fall off of. Failing organizations are more likely to select women CEOs than successful companies. In such situations, the female leader is often seen as a "change" or "something to shake up the status quo." Crisis situations are more likely to need interpersonal skills and have relationship building needs, which female leaders are perceived to be better at.

Within the MCU, we can see that during the five-year gap period after Thanos has destroyed half the population of the universe. This is of course an extreme crisis situation, and one could see this as a failure in part of the leadership of superheroes at the time. Captain America, Iron Man, Thor, and even the Hulk drift away from the Avengers and the potential of leading the superheroes of Earth. Black Widow is the person who is the leader during this time, picking up the pieces after a crisis. Like the glass cliff scenario, a female leader is in charge during this time of crisis. The films offer no guidance on why Black Widow becomes the leader other than that most of the male candidates for leader are not available to lead. We do see her engaging in a relationship building role, connecting with other heroes and relevant groups or nations such as Wakanda. Our glimpse of this is unfortunately quite brief, although it seems she is doing a good job in the situation. As a solution to this situation comes about, however, Black Widow moves more toward the background with the more traditional and male leaders such as Captain America and Iron Man taking back control. Black Widow doesn't seem to get much credit for keeping the world together during those five years unfortunately.

When women are given leadership roles, there can be challenges related to the power and authority they possess. This can be seen in the roles they are given. Research by Glass and Cook (2016) found that only 13% of women started as CEO while also being chair of the board of directors compared to 50% of men. Women often lack the authority that comes from holding both roles at once. They also often receive less support from board members and other leaders, including sexism and exclusion from important formal and informal meetings. Thus, their authority is undermined and their support is less than most male leaders.

Existing research points to the significant challenges our world unfortunately has for female leaders, despite the fact that women are as effective as men in leadership roles (Gipson et al., 2017). In the next part of this chapter, we will specifically highlight the ways we can help women leaders to be successful.

## How to Help Create (Her)oes

With what we know about challenges faced by female leaders, we can use this knowledge to be leaders who help to reduce these challenges and help our organizations to have the (Her)oes they need.

An important first step is to understand the implicit theories we and others may have that keep women with leadership potential from being identified and selected for leadership roles. When looking at people in our organizations with leadership potential, we should not only look for those with agentic and dominant personalities. They may fit our vision of what leaders are like, but that doesn't mean they will be the best people to actually be leaders. And with this, we also need to make sure we don't look at such personalities differently for men and women. A person who is acting assertively should be assessed the same regardless of their gender. It shouldn't be seen as a positive for men and a negative for women. We need to step back when making these judgments about leadership potential and make sure they are not rooted in gender stereotypes.

We also need to be more thoughtful in how we identify those with leadership potential. When we don't have clear standards of what leadership traits or experiences are important in our own organization, we will be more likely to fall back on these implicit theories that discriminate. What makes a good middle manager? Vice president? CEO? If we create standards based on our own organizational needs and environment, we are more likely to find people who actually fit the needs rather than people who meet leadership stereotypes.

Another important step is to make sure that women in our organizations have opportunities to be leaders and work across gender lines. Research by Finseraas, Johnsen, Kotsadam, and Torsvik (2016) looked at how female candidates were perceived for squad leader roles in the Norwegian Armed Forces. Female candidates were perceived as less suited for the role, but if a male soldier worked with a female soldier in an intense collaborative experience, these discriminatory perceptions disappeared. The soldiers discriminated against a theoretical female candidate they didn't know, but when they had experiences working with competent female candidates, they saw those candidates as equal to male candidates. When people get to experience working with female leaders, the idea of a female leader becomes more real and acceptable. Making sure women have the same opportunities as men to lead even small projects or work groups can help to normalize female leaders in an organization. While we haven't seen this approach in the MCU, in the comic book universe, the Avengers have had at times a rotating chairman of the team role. Such a role could provide leadership opportunities for all members of the team including female members.

When we make female leaders a normal part of organizational life rather than an exception, we are likely to reduce the tendency to have female leaders be just the leader turned to in crisis, times of bad performance or when we need to "shake things up." Certain female leaders may in fact have the relationship building skills needed to be effective during a crisis (Glass & Cook, 2016), but then we should be selecting for those skills rather than just having a woman fill the role. Even in such cases we need to better acknowledge that leadership failure in such situations has as much or more to do with the negative situation and context as the person in the role. We don't want such times to be the only shot a female employee with leadership potential gets a chance to lead.

Lastly, we need to make sure women feel like they will be supported in leadership roles and given the authority and power male job holders do. As had been mentioned previously, women can have a lower desire to seek leadership roles because they feel like they will not have power even in such a role. Research by Goodwin et al. (2020) found that while women have a lower feeling of sense of power for a potential leadership role, if the organization can help to show that they will actually have power in the role (through testimonials or the job description) that sense of power becomes the same for both genders. This in turn makes women more likely to seek the leadership role offered. For our own organizations, stories of successful previous female leaders in the role or similar roles could help female organization members see the potential for personal success in the role. A team like the Avengers may want to highlight the successful leadership of Black Widow so that other women with leadership potential in the future can see the kind of (her)o leader they can be. Organizations also need to make sure those female leaders actually get the support they need, including leadership development programs that fit their particular needs and supportive mentors.

## Summary

When we consider who can be a successful leader, we need to make sure that our beliefs about leaders don't disqualify worthy candidates, as happens too often for women in our world. This leads to less female leaders than there should be, as seen in CEOs in our world and leadership positions in the MCU. This chapter looked to describe the nature of this issue and offer some strategies to reduce it. We want our (her)o leaders to flourish, not be relegated to supporting roles.

We began this chapter by showing the significance of the issue in our own world, with women making up almost half of the workforce in the United States but not being anywhere near that proportion of CEOs in the Fortune 500. This deficiency is found as well globally in business. We also see it in the MCU.

This lack of women in higher level roles has been called the "glass ceiling," with women's progress up organizational hierarchies stopped at lower levels.

One major reason for this issue is implicit theories we have about who should be a leader, with common perceptions of this focused on traits and characteristics that fit with male stereotypes. Thus, we look for leaders who are confident and assertive but can penalize women who show these aspects that are not part of female stereotypes. This is despite the fact that research finds women and men to perform at similar performance levels when leaders (Gipson et al., 2017). Women may also end up feeling leadership roles are not for them and that they will not gain the amount of power male leaders get.

Even when women get an opportunity to lead, they are often put in difficult situations where the chance of failure is high and organizations are in crisis, an idea known as "the glass cliff." We see this in the MCU with Black Widow being in charge of the Avengers during the five-year gap period. These situations are often even more precarious as women are not given the same support male leaders are given such as board of director support, and they may experience undermining and exclusion due to sexist attitudes.

With all these challenges, it is important we as leaders support female leaders and those with leadership potential. The first way to do this is to understand implicit theories and how they can impact who we see as having leadership potential. We can reduce this by having clear standards of what makes a leader successful and what characteristics are valuable in our own organization.

We then need to make sure that women have the opportunity to be leaders, both in large important roles and smaller opportunities. Women in leadership roles help them to gain relevant experiences as well as show others in the organization that women can be good leaders and women in leadership positions are normal. With these opportunities must come appropriate support and authority so they can be successful.

This chapter helped us consider the issue of women not getting a chance to succeed in leadership roles and how we can help to reduce this problem. We need to be the hero leaders who help our (her)oes to thrive as leaders in our organizations.

Chapter 11

# I Can Do This All Day: Steve Rogers, Servant Leader

From the very beginning of his journey, Steve Rogers has been focused on service, even before becoming Captain America. Steve Rogers sees no glory in war as what motivates him to join the fight in World War II is to help the little guy. Steve Rogers cannot just sit back and watch a bully succeed even when that bully commands the Axis powers. This is the essence of Captain America, someone who sees something wrong and tries to correct it. His defining moment as a character is when he leaps on a grenade to protect his fellow soldiers during his early training days despite not having any superpowers. Rogers does this because he wants to serve people.

Leaders are often described as influencing others to get things done. But in many situations, leaders must provide support to their followers so that the followers can accomplish their shared goals. Without the support of a leader, many followers cannot accomplish their goals. In this chapter, we will look at the concept of leaders as both influencer and servant. We will look at the characteristics of a servant leader and a model of servant leadership. Finally, we'll talk about how you can become a servant leader in your organization.

## What Makes a Servant Leader?

Leadership is often seen as making followers do what you expect them to do. Greenleaf (1970) reframes this idea and indicates that a leader's natural inclination may be to serve people first so that they may develop and grow. Thus, rather than the leader drawing out the work from followers, it is followers who are aided in their work by the leader. Whether it's before he gets the serum, when he's fighting in World War II, or when he's facing intergalactic threats, Captain America puts his followers before himself.

You might wonder how does a leader serve his followers? Spencer (2002) identifies 10 characteristics of the servant leader:

1) *Listening* – Servant leaders listen before they speak, allowing their followers the space to speak their minds. Even when Captain America has conflict with Iron Man, he lets Tony to speak his mind.

Leaders Assemble! Leadership in the MCU, 71–76
Copyright © 2022 by Gordon B. Schmidt and Sy Islam
Published under exclusive license by Emerald Publishing Limited
doi:10.1108/978-1-80117-670-520221011

2) *Empathy* – Servant leaders look at the perspective of their own followers first. Often, servant leaders try to validate the experiences of their followers to address their followers' needs more effectively. Captain America cares deeply for his followers. Before he asks Sam Wilson to join his cause he checks to make sure that Sam is comfortable donning the Falcon uniform. Steve knows what Sam has been through and recognizes the cost of putting on the uniform again.

3) *Healing* – Servant leaders care about their followers' health and well-being. Many strive to help their followers with personal issues that may be considered outside the scope of work. Steve goes above and beyond to heal his friend Bucky Barnes after Bucky has been brainwashed to become the Winter Soldier. Steve makes sure to find a place for Bucky in Wakanda where he can heal after the trauma he experienced.

4) *Awareness* – Servant leaders are highly aware of the environment in which they function. This includes physical spaces, social situations, and the internal politics of a culture. Steve knows when the mood has changed, as evidenced by the "elevator fight." Steve enters an elevator full of people who were his friends but that he now realizes are Hydra agents.

5) *Persuasion* – Persuasion is consistent communication that is focused on helping the individual change. Steve is committed to helping his friend Bucky Barnes change over time. He never wavers in his support of Bucky even in the face of opposition from his fellow heroes. Steve does not back down from his position and knows he has to persuade others to his line of thinking.

6) *Foresight* – Foresight is a leader's ability to discern what will happen in the future based on current events. Given his experience in multiple warzones, Captain America knows when his enemies are ready for a fight. His battle acumen is shown in his fight in the elevator with the undercover Hydra agents. As Steve is leaving SHIELD in an elevator, he watches a group of SHIELD agents he fought with verbally earlier all enter. He grows suspicious and realizes that he needs to be ready to fight because these men are not to be trusted. A good leader has this type of foresight.

7) *Conceptualization* – Conceptualization is the process by which the leader sets the vision and mission for the organization. Captain America's ability to conceptualize or create a vision for an organization is evidenced by his leadership during the Battle of New York. Once Steve Rogers takes command, he is able to identify what each Avengers team member needs to do. Captain America knows how to organize team members of various power levels across a massive battlefield to win a fight. It is Captain America's ability to create a clear plan for the Avengers that saves the day.

8) *Stewardship* – Stewardship is about the responsibility of the leader to manage their people and the organization. One of Captain America's central questions is how he can best serve his ideal. Starting in the First Avenger, Captain America takes his role as a protector of people seriously. From his rescue of the 107th infantry to his leadership of the Avengers, Captain America puts his people first. Even when he breaks away to begin his own faction of Avengers in Civil War, the reasons are based in his stewardship of the organization.

9) *Commitment to the Growth of People* – Servant leaders are committed to treating their followers as unique individuals and helping them to develop their skills. Captain America is focused on this among his Avengers teammates as well. When Steve works with Natasha Romanoff (Black Widow), he focuses on her ability to improve and get better. When running with Sam Wilson, before they have even become friends, Steve Rogers pushes Sam to perform and do better. This is a consistent theme across Steve's relationships with all the Avengers. He encourages Natasha to leave the red in her ledger behind, to help reform Wanda Maximoff and the Vision. Beyond institutions, Steve is committed to people.

10) *Building Community* – Servant leaders don't just commit to building individuals; they are committed to building groups of people who believe in something greater than themselves. Steve Rogers builds a community through his commitment to the Avengers. This community follows him whether it's to become a faction of the Avengers opposed to the Sokovia Accords or battle Thanos on a distant world. Steve trusts that his community will be there for him when he needs them.

These 10 traits embody the characteristics of a servant leader. Let's contrast the servant leadership of Steve Rogers with the narcissistic leadership of Loki and Thanos. Loki's initial goal when he has a Chitauri army at his disposal is to conquer humanity and turn them into slaves. Loki is looking to disempower his followers, whereas a servant leader like Steve Rogers is looking to empower his followers. Thanos may not be as extreme as Loki in his attempt to enslave humanity, but he is only committed to his vision of the future regardless of the costs to his followers. Steve Rogers would jump on a grenade for his fellow soldiers, whereas Thanos sacrifices his adopted daughter Gamora, for an opportunity to achieve his goals. Thanos embodies the characteristics of a toxic leader who will do anything to achieve his goal (Milosevic, Maric, & Lancar, 2020). Thanos' followers are often sacrificed for his goals whereas Steve Rogers puts himself in harm's way first.

Leaders across many organizations attempt to help their followers perform more effectively. When you are considering the servant leadership approach, think about how you can behave according to these traits. Consider your experiences with a leader who showed the type of care we described above. This could be your CEO or a departmental leader. Even a peer can embody these servant leadership traits. People who know that their leaders are working for them are often more committed followers.

## Will Followers Follow the Servant?

One of the common lay assumptions of leadership is that people follow strong leaders who use a command-and-control approach to leadership. When we imagine a leader, we don't always see someone who helps us but someone who gives us orders. This is one of the many things that makes Captain America such an interesting case study for servant leadership. Steve Rogers was trained in a command-and-control model of military leadership, yet he remains committed to servant leadership. One reason Captain America has been a successful servant leader is because of his followers' willingness to listen to him. There are a few lessons we can take from Captain America about why people follow him based on his servant leadership behaviors.

Liden et al. (2014) developed a model of servant leadership that included several important servant leadership behaviors. There is some overlap of these behaviors with Spencer's (2002) traits discussed above. The key differences in servant leadership behaviors include behaving ethically, putting followers first, empowering, and creating value for the community. Here's some ways that Captain America embodies these servant leadership behaviors.

First, Captain America never asks his followers or team members to do anything that he himself would not do. Captain America is the first person to take risks. During the events of Avengers Endgame, Captain America joins Tony Stark and Bruce Banner on a time travel journey. Captain America also stands up to Thanos at the height of his power with the Infinity Gauntlet. He gives his teammates the time to join the battle. He never puts others in harm's way or avoids responsibility for a task that he finds unappealing. Captain America acts on the servant leadership principle of putting his followers first.

Second, Captain America's followers realize that he is committed to their well-being. Steve Rogers consistently shows that he cares about each team member as individuals. During the first Avengers mission, he checks in with Bruce Banner about his potential to turn into the Hulk. If you are on Steve Rogers' team you know that he'll be there for you. When Steve drops everything to stop the Black Panther from harming Bucky Barnes, it's the most potent evidence to others in Steve's camp like Natasha Romanoff and Sam Wilson that he will always show up when they need him. It is especially impressive that Steve is able to get someone like Natasha Romanoff on his side considering her cynical attitude toward agencies and teams. Natasha has been in the spy game where loyalties shift constantly. Her commitment to Steve Rogers shows how powerful his servant leadership truly is.

Part of the reason that servant leadership works in favor of Captain America is because of Captain America's authenticity. Authentic leaders are ones who express their true selves to their followers (van Dierendonck & Nuijten, 2011), as we discussed in Chapter 7. Authenticity and servant leadership are often linked to one another. Servant leaders are often more effective when they are authentic. In many ways, this is Captain America's greatest strength, you always know where you stand in relation to Steve Rogers, and if you're on his side, he's always willing to serve you.

Captain America also has a sensitivity to others that highlights his servant leadership. He makes sure to protect Bucky Barnes by sending him to Wakanda to receive treatment for his damaged psyche and cybernetic arm. Despite being on the run, Steve Rogers' idealism as Captain America and his ability to conceptualize the true mission of why superhumans would want to be Avengers keeps his followers with him.

A core element of servant leadership is ethical behavior. Out of all the Avengers, Steve Rogers represents the hero who most often follows what he believes to be right. His code of ethics means that he makes choices that are guided by his principles. Despite his military training's focus on obedience, Captain America always does what he believes is right. In his first adventure, Steve Rogers rejects his commanding officers' orders to save the 107th battalion. Steve Rogers knows what's right and he makes sure that as Captain America he follows through on that purpose, even if that purpose puts him at odds with others.

Ultimately, this means that Captain America embodies the behaviors of a servant leader. His idealism and commitment to his ethics creates a level of comfort for his followers to agree to follow him through whatever danger arises. Captain America embodies Liden et al.'s (2014) servant leader behaviors. Research indicates that effective servant leaders can lead teams effectively (Sousa & Van Dierendonck, 2016) as well as organizations (de Waal & Sivro, 2012). If you want to find a way to make your organization more effective, servant leadership could be effective.

## Can a Servant Change the World?

Most leadership theories are focused on helping organizations perform more effectively with the focus on organizational capacity and improved outcomes for employees. In other words, can leaders make the world better within their organizations and for the ones who work there? However, servant leadership includes an understanding of the impact that a leader may have on society. When we think of superheroes, we often think of individuals with incredible powers that can change the world. Servant leadership theory posits that leaders can change the world. Steve Rogers is a strong example of a leader who can change the world.

As a symbol during World War II, Captain America not only serves in the army on the frontlines but also helps to galvanize the movement against the Nazi invasion back home. His idealism is communicated through newsreel footage and his victories. When Captain America returns from being frozen in the ice, he changes the world again by leading the Avengers, the world's first team of superheroes.

After sacrificing himself to stop Hydra in World War II, Captain America remains a potent memory that inspires many others. Steve Rogers serves as the inspiration for the Avengers Initiative concocted by Nick Fury and Agent Phil Coulson. A servant leader can be a beacon to others on their teams and have a much longer lasting impact than previously imagined. The combination of Steve Rogers' authentic leadership and servant leadership showed his followers that he stood by what he believed and that he always did what was best for them. These two traits made Steve Rogers a potent figure for those who were more cynical like Black Widow and Hawkeye. Even powerful figures like the Ancient One trust Steve Rogers. When Steve requests the time stone from the Ancient One, despite some hesitation, she gives it to him. The combination of knowing that he serves others and that he is authentic in his leadership makes him someone that even god-like beings can trust.

Think about your own experiences in the workplace. As an employee in an organization, you may be inspired by the service of your fellow leaders. A leader may provide you with emotional support during a time of need or provide you with a learning opportunity so that you may personally grow. Research has shown that leaders who engage in servant leadership behaviors can have a positive impact on employees' experience of work (Guillaume, Honeycutt, & Savage-Austin, 2013). Your behavior as a leader can have an impact on your colleagues or subordinates' experience of the workplace. Providing emotional support or truly listening to a colleague or follower can make an enormous difference in how they experience their day-to-day work. You may not become a symbol at the level of Captain America, but your behavior on the job can provide needed relief to employees.

One of the hurdles in becoming a servant leader is the common belief that a leader is above their followers or subordinates. If you are considering following servant leadership to develop your own leadership capabilities, then it's in your best interest to reflect on what you offer to your team. Steve Rogers never hesitated in serving others because it was his passion, it was how he knew to lead. Captain America knew that no matter what the situation, he would always find a way to do the right thing.

## Summary

Leaders can do more than just command; they can provide support to their followers. In this chapter, we discussed some of the traits that make a leader a servant leader, looking to the Captain America and the Avengers films as a source of examples. Leaders can provide emotional support by listening and behaving in an empathetic manner with their followers. Leaders and those who engage in leadership behavior can create a better work environment with their coworkers by being committed to their individual growth and well-being. Persuasion is also a key characteristic of servant leaders, they must be able to persuade others to their way of thinking in order to lead. Followers need servant leaders who have a strong sense of awareness of their environments in a variety of levels (physical, emotional, political) to make effective decisions for their followers and themselves.

Effective servant leaders using foresight can communicate a clear vision to their followers about the future of their organization. Servant leaders must also maintain high ethical standards to maintain their authenticity with their followers. Servant leaders who maintain their ethical stance and balance organizational outcomes with employee well-being are the most effective.

Finally, in this section, we discussed the impact of servant leaders. Unlike other leadership theories where the focus may not extend beyond the organizations in which leaders operate, servant leadership views the impact of the leader as being an impact felt on the world. By empowering employees, treating them ethically, and engaging in a healing process with them, servant leaders help these employees to achieve more. This process of stewardship creates an impact on the communities in which servant leaders' function.

Servant leaders must think carefully about how they conduct themselves. Without a careful approach, servant leaders may appear to be micromanagers who are overly concerned in the affairs of their employees. Effective servant leaders know how to balance their care and concern for their followers, their organizations, and their community to deliver the greatest impact.

Chapter 12

# Avengers Assemble: Forming Your Team Like a Leader

One of the early connections between Marvel Cinematic Universe movies was Nick Fury talking to heroes and trying to recruit them for the "Avengers Initiative." This started out as a last-minute addition to "Iron Man," just an Easter egg to fans of what could happen in future films (Wetzel & Wetzel, 2020). It of course became something much larger, as Fury's actions continued, leading to the creation of the Avengers team.

For any organization, it is crucial to create the right team for what the organization is trying to accomplish. Leaders can be an important part of this process at multiple stages. As we saw across movies, Fury worked to recruit heroes to be part of the Avengers. He needed to figure out which heroes were relevant to an Avengers team and select the right ones. Finally, Fury needed to keep the team together, as heroes leaving would mean the team could not perform as well as it could or even function at all (as we can see in some of the later films). None of this is an easy task, as each Avenger has a unique and strong personality, with different needs and wants for a team.

In this chapter, we'll talk about how leaders can play an important role in putting together their team in an organization. We'll be using the classic Human Resources model of Attraction–Selection–Attrition (Schneider, Goldstein, & Smith, 1995) to illustrate how a leader can impact who wants to join a team, who gets invited to join, and who ultimately stays. We'll look at the recruiting of the Avengers, and both Professor X and Magneto recruiting for their own teams.

## Getting Them to Accept the Call to be a Hero

In order to put a team together, a leader and organization needs to be able to recruit relevant people to be interested in the team. This is the "Attraction" step of the Attraction–Selection–Attrition model (Schneider et al., 1995). How do people become attracted to a particular organization? One major aspect is person-organization (P-O) fit, which is the perceived fit between a person's characteristics, values, and goals with those of the organization itself (Kristof, 1996). When a person feels they are similar to an organization in these areas, they will have a greater

Leaders Assemble! Leadership in the MCU, 77–82
Copyright © 2022 by Gordon B. Schmidt and Sy Islam
Published under exclusive license by Emerald Publishing Limited
doi:10.1108/978-1-80117-670-520221012

attraction to joining the organization. This P-O fit can also relate to a person's goals. If the person feels the organization will help them reach their goals, they will be more attracted to the organization as well. The characteristics of an organization will often be shaped by the organization's founder and prominent leaders, so they are essentially setting the tone for these variables that will act to attract people with similar characteristics (Schneider et al., 1995).

In Marvel films, we can see many examples of this from leaders. As we talked about in a previous chapter, Professor Xavier and Magneto offer different appeals to those mutants whom they try to recruit. Professor X is more likely to talk about the values of learning to control one's powers and working to help humanity. Magneto is more likely to talk about people using those powers to gain more power and having the goal of mutants having control over nonmutant humanity. For a particular person with mutant powers, one of these messages is likely more appealing and thus attracts them to Xavier's or Magneto's team. We see this in "X-2," with Pyro, who goes to Xavier's school but finds Magneto's message more appealing so he quits and joins the Brotherhood of Mutants instead.

The recruiting of the Avengers includes many examples of this attraction step. Fury works for a secret organization (SHIELD), and the Avengers are a new idea. People he talks to are unlikely to have existing feelings about either organization or know what they are about. So Fury needs to introduce both organizations to the heroes he meets and help show why they should be appealing to that particular hero. Fury appeals to Tony Stark's desire to make the world a better place. He also helps Stark with his heart condition. When Bruce Banner is recruited, the appeal focuses on his science knowledge and value (which Banner provides) vs. the fact he can turn into the Hulk (which Banner sees as a curse, not a benefit). Fury frames this new Avenger team as something that will take on missions others cannot to help the world. Thus, he suggests an important mission people can get behind.

As a leader, you often will have influence on the things that make your team or organization appealing. Do you have a mission that people care about? Does your company have meaningful values? How can the organization help members to reach their own personal goals? These factors together will help create better P-O fit and attract relevant people to the organization. Of course, these things must be more than just talk. If an organization appears to have appealing factors but in fact does not, they will lose those talented individuals over time, as we will discuss later in the attrition section. As we saw with Nick Fury, relevant individuals may not even be familiar with your organization and what it does – leaders will be an important part of sharing that knowledge.

## Selecting the Right Heroes

In many situations, organizations need to make choices on who to select among multiple candidates for a role. Does a team need both Ant-man and the Wasp, one of them, or are their skill sets not relevant for the particular role? Leaders will often be part of the process of figuring out what positions we need in the team or organization and in ultimately selecting the best candidate for the job. The "Selection" step of the Attraction–Selection–Attrition model (Schneider et al., 1995) is all about this process of organizations selecting the right person and candidates deciding to select the right organization for them. While organizations may need a range of different skills for all their different roles, organizations will often have particular characteristics and values they tend to want across employees. Think about job postings you yourself have seen. Have you seen organizations talking about wanting "team players" or "outside the box thinkers" or people who are "bold?" These are all personality characteristics or values organizations may suggest they want employees to have. If these help determine who gets hired over time, the organization will ultimately have more employees with the relevant characteristics.

So how should an organization select the right candidate? In looking across a number of studies using a technique called a meta-analysis, Schmidt and Hunter (1998) found that the most valid methods for selecting people in general are work sample tests, structured interviews, and intelligence measurements. Work sample tests involve a person doing tasks that they will do on the job, so for an Avenger who might be fighting a super villain (or a simulation of one like the X-men's Danger Room). For structured interviews, the same set of job-related questions are asked to each candidate for the position. These structured interviews are consistently found to be more valid and effective than unstructured interviews, where the interviewers ask whatever questions they like. While an unstructured interview may feel to interviewers like they can gain more insight by asking unique questions per candidate, research suggests that it can just lead to bias and makes the interviews of different candidates less comparable. Intelligence is generally found to help people learn quicker and perform better, so it is not surprising it is a good predictor of job success. Take a look at a team like the Avengers and you will find quite a few very intelligent people, such as Tony Stark and Bruce Banner.

When we look to Marvel films, we can see some real deficiencies in selection processes. We don't see a consistent method of evaluating who are the best people to join a team like the Avengers. In "Iron Man 2," it is directly mentioned that Tony Stark actually failed the Avengers selection test due to his personality. Whether or not the test is appropriate for the job, it's a red flag that Fury asked him to join the Avenger anyway. If we don't think the test works (or even better, have validity evidence), we should stop using it, not just make exceptions when we feel like it. The Avengers is made up of people with unique skill sets, but that doesn't mean we should pick people without clear criteria. SHIELD itself seems to have a selection problem, as the downfall of the organizations happened due to too many villainous Hydra agents getting hired by the organizations and taking over. They really needed more rigorous screening testing to filter out such unsuitable candidates!

The criteria for selection by Professor Xavier seem a bit clearer, but complications lie below the surface. Xavier's School for Gifted Youngsters seems to have the basic criteria of selecting people with mutant powers. So nonmutants need not apply. However, it seems unlikely Xavier selects all mutants. Being able to grow a beard quickly is probably not a mutation that gets you a spot at the school. There seems to be some power level or level of distress of mutation that is needed to be invited. And for the X-men team itself, there is a limited number of active members at a time. Your power needs to be of a considerable level that is relevant for fighting villains. The X-men films don't give clear ideas on what these criteria are, and there are several instances of people basically showing up (e.g., Wolverine) and being added to the team almost right away. Not a great way to make sure a person is the right fit for the job!

Note that selection is a two-way street, an organization may offer a position, but the candidate may decline. Just like an organization has multiple candidates, a candidate may have multiple potential job offers. Perceptions of the selection process are relevant, as those with a positive perception of the selection process as fair are more likely to look at the organizations positively and accept a job offer (Hausknecht, Day, & Thomas, 2004). Interviews and work samples are perceived as the most favorable of selection methods.

As a leader, you can impact this selection process in many important ways. Leaders will often have a say in selection methods used, and we would recommend you help your organization to use the valid methods discussed (making sure they fit with the laws and regulation of your own environment). And you need to take the methods seriously and use them to inform a decision! If you never take into account structured interview or work sample data in the people you choose, others in the organization are likely to follow your lead. You also need to make sure selection processes are seen in a positive light by applicants or you may lose good candidates. Much of what we talked about in attraction applies here as well – people who perceived a high fit with the organization's values and goals are going to be more likely to accept a job offer when given. As a leader you play a major part in setting those goals and showing those values.

## I Quit! A Hero Has Left the Team

Every organization will have people who leave at some point. This is the "Attrition" step of the Attraction–Selection–Attrition model (Schneider et al., 1995), where people leave the organization (also known as "turnover") often due to feelings they don't fit with the organization (or potentially get fired due to their actions not fitting with organizational values or goals). Turnover is a real problem for organizations, with research finding that higher rates of turnover relate to lower levels of performance at an organization, especially when people are deciding to leave themselves versus being fired (Park & Shaw, 2013). People leaving the organization can be detrimental, especially when it involves high performers.

The common idea that people quit jobs due to bad bosses has some research support in that satisfaction with a supervisor does predict lower turnover, albeit it is a relatively weak predictor compared to other factors such as job satisfaction and organizational commitment (Griffeth, Hom, & Gaertner, 2000). So a good leader can help, but won't keep someone in the organization if they are not generally satisfied with the job or committed to it. Some research suggests good leadership can actually lead people to leave an organization, as the strong professional development received from their leader makes them more desirable to other companies (Raghuram, Gajendran, Liu, & Somaya, 2017)! Even in such a case though those leaving are more likely to feel goodwill toward the organization and thus recommend the organization to others. This effect is stronger when the leader makes an effort to retain the person and change their mind on quitting.

So leaders can have a big role in convincing people they want to remain in the organization and feel a sense of belonging. As we see in X-men films, Wolverine often bristles against being a member of the X-men and being a member of the team. We might see him as feeling his P-O fit is lacking with the X-men, who seem more clean-cut and rule-following than him. He tries to quit or denies being an X-men at various times. Professor Xavier plays an important role in making Wolverine see his actual fit with the team and that his values are actually in alignment with the X-men. This work with Wolverine builds his connection with the team, and Wolverine ultimately becomes a very committed member of the team, willing to make major sacrifices to help the team's goals.

Nick Fury also tries to keep Avenger members on the team. When the team first fights with Loki in "Marvel's The Avengers," disagreements in the team are exacerbated, and the team wants to quit and go their separate ways. It is Fury, as their leader, who reminds the team of their importance and that they have a mission no one else can accomplish. He appeals to their values that are in common, not their other characteristics that may be not. Fury helps keep the team together. Good leaders help people to see where they fit in an organization and why it is a place they should stay.

## Summary

Leaders play an important role in putting together the team that works with them. Leaders need to act in an intentional and careful manner to make sure they put together the right team and do what is needed to keep that team together.

We examined elements of how this happens through the idea of the Attraction–Select–Attrition model, highlighting how people first get interested in an organization, get selected into it, and then potentially leave the organization. Leaders are crucial in all three areas.

The first stage of attraction is related to recruiting people for an organization. How do we get people interested in the organization and want to be part of it? One big factor is P-O fit, how much a person feels like their own characteristics and goals fit with the organization. Leaders help shape the goals and characteristics of an organization that become the elements that attract people to it. They also often act as models and communicators of those values and goals. Make sure you as a leader think about how you show those values and goals, as just giving a paycheck is rarely enough to keep a person for long.

The second stage of selection is deciding who we want to actually be a member of the organization. If we have an appealing image and goals, we are likely to get more people interested than available roles. How do we decide who is best for a role? We highlighted that work sample tests, structured interviews, and intelligence are the most valid predictors of job success. As leaders, we want to encourage such methods for use. We also need to consider that selection is a two-way street, as the best candidates will often have options to work with other organizations or join other superhero teams. If we want Wolverine on our side, we need to make sure we communicate why he should be an X-men, not an Avenger. As a leader, we need to convince him.

The third stage of attrition relates to the simple fact that people leave organizations over time. People leaving hurts the performance of our organizations and can happen because of a perceived lack of fit. As leaders, we need to support our subordinates and remind them why our organization is the right fit for them. We don't want our best performers to leave and join the Brotherhood of Mutants or even worse, our top competitor!

As a leader, we are an important part of the selection process. We need to make sure we use our leadership powers for good – finding the right people, getting them to join our team, and staying together even when times are tough, whether it be fighting Ultron or dealing with a difficult client.

Our powers as a leader CAN save the day, we just need to make sure we understand when and how to use them. Our final chapter will tie the previous chapters all together to help you do that.

Chapter 13

# How You, True Believer, Can Lead Like a Superhero: Some General Takeaways on Leadership

Every superhero movie ultimately ends. Good films leave you feeling excited and looking forward to what happens next. The goals of this final chapter are similar. Across our other chapters we've used examples across Marvel films to introduce and illustrate research-supported concepts that help you to be a good leader. The world needs more and better leaders. We can all improve as leaders and have an impact on our world. With the knowledge and insight from this book's chapters, you should be prepared to be the superhero leader your organization or group needs.

In this final chapter, we help to summarize that learning and give you directly actionable steps to take next. Each chapter did include advice on how to learn from the Marvel Cinematic Universe (MCU) examples and research-supported concepts discussed. This chapter though gives you condensed summaries that are focused on how you apply what has been learned. Each previous chapter will have its main points for your own use as a leader emphasized. We've also given a title to each summary that emphasizes that main point and takeaway.

So here are our 11 recommendations for how this book can inform your practice of leadership today and in your future.

## Leaders Need to Consider What Their Power is and How They Use it

As we discussed in Chapter 2, to function effectively, organizations must maintain a healthy leadership pipeline. Leaders don't reign forever and for an organization to stay on top, it must be able to develop new leadership talent. Organizations must be proactive in recruiting leaders, selecting leaders, and promoting leaders throughout their organization. Organizations should treat leadership transitions as important events which can help determine the future of the organization. By selecting and promoting the right leaders, the organization ensures its future success.

**Leaders Assemble! Leadership in the MCU, 83–90**
**Copyright © 2022 by Gordon B. Schmidt and Sy Islam**
**Published under exclusive license by Emerald Publishing Limited**
**doi:10.1108/978-1-80117-670-520221013**

Organizations can begin by recruiting for a talented pool of potential leaders both within and outside the organization. When searching for leadership talent, peer referrals, professional societies, and social media can all be leveraged to expand the talent pool. You can select a potential leader from this talent pool by using objective assessments of leadership competencies of personality. You can keep your leadership pipeline flowing by monitoring potential leaders on their leadership competencies.

When in a leadership position, you should consider what sources of power you can draw upon. Do people follow you because they like you? Do they follow your lead because of information you know or specialized expertise that you have? Do they follow you because of your position or the potential rewards you can provide? Or do you force people to follow you? Understanding your sources of power can help you maintain and develop your leadership role. A good leader knows the power that they have and how to leverage it.

## In Many Situations Sharing Leadership is How We Do Best

A discussed in Chapter 3, teams sometimes need to learn how to share leadership among one another. While we often imagine that teams need a singular, assigned leader, research suggests that teams using a shared leadership approach can be just as effective as a traditional hierarchical leadership arrangement. A strong team can utilize all the skills of its team members, especially leadership skills.

Before your team can utilize shared leadership, make sure that your team sees itself as a team with a consistent membership. Highlight the interdependence of the work you and your team do. Make sure that your team members know that they need each other to get the work done. As a leader in a shared leadership environment, you should monitor both task-oriented and relational behaviors. A good leader establishes the boundaries and goals for their team and manages the relationships among team members.

A team with strong shared leadership is often adaptable in a variety of work contexts. Build up your team member's individual competencies and rotate the leadership role across your teammates and you can build a flexible team that can handle working within your group and with others. Shared leaders know that they'll have their chance to lead when their competencies match the situation. There's plenty of leadership to go around!

## Great Leadership is Fostered by Great Mentoring

As discussed in Chapter 4, mentoring can help leaders and protégés. Mentorship programs are an effective way to develop the next generation of leaders by pairing mentors and protégés to one another. Mentors provide perspective and guidance to protégés while protégés help to keep mentors abreast of what's happening within the organization. A good leader needs to help foster effective mentoring relationships with their protégés.

When looking for a mentor, protégés need to find a mentor who they feel can provide them with the best guidance. Find a mentor who knows what you want to know and can guide you to the right career path. When serving as a mentor, be ready to share your knowledge with a protégé that is looking for what you have to offer. While demographic characteristics might be an attractive way to match mentors and protégés, finding a mentor who can teach what a protégé wants to know is the most important characteristic to match.

Seeking an individual mentor might prove challenging, so you can look for mentors among your peers or even in a group. Peer mentoring can provide deep insight from someone who shares many similarities with you. Group mentoring provides a wealth of knowledge beyond just having a single mentor. Ultimately, any mentoring relationship is about building a shared vision around career goals. With a single mentor, a peer mentor, or a group of mentors, developing a shared vision can benefit your organization and improve performance.

## Conflict Can Help Us Make Better Decisions, But Not When it is Personal

As was discussed in Chapter 5, conflict arises in all situations and a leader needs to be prepared for it. While we as individuals often try to avoid conflict, research suggests that conflict can be good at times. Conflict helps us to share our differing views and potentially come up with better solutions to problems. By sharing and disagreeing on what to do, we gain input that could improve the solution. A good leader needs to help foster this beneficial conflict, encouraging people to share their different opinions and insight on accomplishing organizational objectives.

Where a leader needs to reduce conflict, however, is when it gets personal or is damaging to relationships between people. When conflict turns to being personal and about a person's values and personality, it has a detrimental impact. As a leader you need to steer people away from such personal conflict and make sure the conflict is on tasks, not people.

When there is conflict, a leader needs to help to resolve the conflict and lead their team to a resolution. Collaboration is the best method to resolve conflict as it involves truly understanding the point of disagreement and what people actually want and need. This understanding allows for a solution that better meets everyone's needs rather than splitting down the middle or just picking one person's argument as "correct." A good leader should be striving for collaboration and making sure conflict doesn't interfere with the relationships on a team.

## We Need to Find Ways to Reduce Stress and Not Just Deal with it in the Moment

As we discussed in Chapter 6, leaders play a big part in the stress of their followers, both in terms of leaders' actions and reactions to stressful events. A leader needs to work to reduce stress for followers and make sure stress isn't causing him or her to behave in negative ways.

Self-care is important for a leader. Stress affects us all, and we can't be a good leader when overwhelmed by stress and crisis. We need to acknowledge stress and take action to help to reduce the problem. Too often we depend on reactive strategies to deal with stress like working longer hours or depending on caffeine to keep us going. We need to spend more time developing proactive strategies that build our skills related to dealing with stress, such as time management and relaxation techniques. Most importantly, we need to take action with enactive strategies that help to eliminate sources of stress. Redesigning a job (such as allowing remote work) or changing our environment (like moving closer to our workplace) often takes a lot of time and effort but also has the largest impact on reducing or removing a stressor. Real solutions to our stress take time but really help us to be our best.

Leaders need to help their followers to deal with stress and to help reduce the stress they have. Leaders must be prepared for issues and stress to arise. The best way to deal with a crisis is to be already prepared for such a situation to happen. Consider things that could happen and have a plan. Good leaders in a crisis or stressful situation need to engage in clear and transparent communication. The leader needs to act as a role model showing a calm demeanor focusing on getting through the situation. As a leader, you should be trying to reduce the stressors impacting your followers and ready with plans for negative situations that may arise.

## Being Authentic Helps Us to be Our Best Leader

As discussed in Chapter 7, for us to be the best leader we can be, we need to have self-awareness. A good leader understands his or her own strengths, weaknesses, and preferences. Tony Stark struggles in part because he lacks self-awareness of who he wants to be. Self-awareness can be difficult as we often resist negative information, especially when it relates to something important to our sense of self. Only through hard work and self-reflection can we become more self-aware.

When a person is self-aware, he or she becomes able to be authentic in how he or she presents himself or herself and acts. Being authentic is beneficial to our own well-being and it helps our relationships with others. When we hold back and try to behave in ways we think others want us to be, we often perform worse. To be our best, we need to be authentic.

Authentic leadership builds on the idea of authenticity with a focus on being a good leader. Authentic leaders foster self-awareness among followers and create an environment where everyone can develop. Authentic leaders help others to be authentic as well and thus be the best version of themselves. Thus, authentic leadership can help your team to perform better and behave in ways that best fit with team members' actual preferences and characteristics.

## Leaders Help Groups to Work with Others

As discussed in Chapter 8, leaders need to not only work with their own teams but also work with other teams and organizations. Leaders often work within networks involving teams in the same organization or negotiating with external organizations. Leaders have to manage the external environment to achieve organizational success. When you serve as a leader, you not only serve a function inside your team but you represent and wield power outside of it as well.

The role of an external leader is a key ingredient to much of modern leadership. Leaders must know what the vision for their own team is and then negotiate for that among the real world. Leaders are expected to bring in resources and negotiate favorable terms with other groups and organizations. A leader who can both manage an organization and serve as the mouthpiece for that organization is a formidable force. As a leader, you can craft a vision and implement a plan within your organization. But after the internal work is complete, a true leader knows how to present this vision to the external world.

You can develop these skills of external leadership by focusing on where your experiences have led you as a leader. Reflect on your experiences and limitations. Consider how you can create a vision for your organization that not only includes what your team must do internally but what must be done with external stakeholders. Good leaders know how to manage internal and external relationships. A leader who knows how to exercise their power within a team and outside of a team can truly be successful!

## Leaders Help Followers Understand the World

As discussed in Chapter 9, leaders play a crucial role in helping their followers to understand and interpret what is going on. The world at times can be a confusing and ambiguous place. Leaders explain what events mean for an organization, how followers should think about them, and what behaviors followers should do. When leaders don't do such sensemaking, followers make their own judgments and may act in contradictory ways. When you engage in leadership, you are often making sure people are on the same page and know what to do, whether your team is family members, work colleagues, or superheroes.

This role for leaders of helping people to see the world in a particular way can also extend to how a follower identifies with being part of an organization or group. People who identify strongly with a group will be more likely to put in effort and resources to help the group. They will more strongly support organization missions. As a leader, you have to shape the identity of an organization and how followers see it. If the identity presented is not appealing or meaningful, people will leave for organizations that have such identities. Leaders communicate what the organization's identity is.

Organizational commitment is the degree to which a person desires to remain part of the organization. There are many different reasons why a person might desire to stay. They may want to stay because they feel emotionally connected to the organization. They may stay because they don't feel they have anywhere else to go. They may stay out of a sense of obligation to the organization. Good leaders will act in ways that make followers feel more committed to the organization and want to stay.

## Leaders Come from All Genders

Successful leaders can come from any gender, as we discussed in Chapter 10. Research supports that women and men perform at similar level in leadership roles (Gipson et al., 2017). Despite this, women are underrepresented in leadership roles, especially at higher levels. This can be due to implicit leadership theories that suggest successful leaders have traditionally masculine characteristics. This is a problem for the world and leaves many potential great leaders outside of leadership roles.

As leaders, we need to make sure we work to support female leaders and those with leadership potential. We need to make sure female leaders get chances to succeed and don't only get opportunities in high-risk situations. When working with women and women leaders are common, more women see themselves as potential leaders and step forward. A good leader needs to make sure the people with the best leadership potential get a chance, not just males with those characteristics. Creating clear criteria for what we look for in leadership roles in an organization can help.

## To Lead Sometimes the Best Thing to Do is Serve

As discussed in Chapter 11, a servant leader is one who works to help their subordinates to work and grow. Leaders can play an important role in the development of their subordinates. Leaders are only successful when their subordinates are successful, and a leader who focuses on helping subordinates can truly make an impact.

Leaders wield an enormous amount of power within an organization. Servant leaders focus that power on helping their subordinates get what they need to do their jobs. Leaders who utilize servant leadership and are seen as supportive often attract a more fervent following. As a leader, you can model appropriate behaviors and show subordinates how best to approach challenges.

By focusing on the needs of their followers, servant leaders can create an environment where performance is of the utmost importance while still maintaining strong relationships with subordinates. A good servant leader knows how to utilize their team members and to give them everything they need to perform in the job. Servant leaders listen and create an environment where their subordinates are safe and able to do the work that needs to be done.

Servant leaders keep their subordinates motivated by serving as potent symbols. Leadership involves not only the actions of the leader but the reactions of followers. When followers know that you care about them, they will be more motivated to do the work that needs to be done.

## A Good Leader Needs the Right Team

In Chapter 12, we highlighted that leaders need the right team to succeed. Leaders can play a crucial role in recruiting and selecting members for their own teams. Leaders also need to make sure that team members get their needs fulfilled, otherwise we might lose crucial heroes for our team's success.

Leaders will often be an important part of attracting good candidates to an organization. They will help potential team members see the organization as a good fit for joining. Leaders set the tone for the mission of an organization and its values. Potential team members need to see the team as appealing.

Leaders will often need to choose between multiple candidates for a role. Leaders shouldn't just go with their "gut" or the like in making decisions, they should use valid selection tools like work sample tests and structured interviews. A superhero looking "cool" doesn't mean he or she will be the best team member. Leaders also set the tone of what selection criteria matter – if you ignore the selection tool data, you are signaling to others to do the same.

Finally, leaders need to keep team members engaged and satisfied. Other chapters have spoken related to this topic as well, but it is crucial in putting together your team. As a leader you want to instill a sense of belonging in team members. Your team needs to stay together so it can work together and ultimately "save the day" for your organization.

## Summary

In this last chapter, we summarized actionable lessons from each of the preceding chapters. Each of these lessons can be used when you engage in leadership. Those lessons were:

- Leaders Need to Consider What Their Power Is and How They Use It
- In Many Situations, Sharing Leadership Is How We Do Best
- Great Leadership Is Fostered by Great Mentoring
- Conflict Can Help Us Make Better Decisions But Not When It Is Personal
- We Need to Find Ways to Reduce Stress and Not Just Deal With It in the Moment
- Being Authentic Helps Us to Be Our Best Leader
- Leaders Help Groups to Work With Others
- Leaders Help Followers Understand the World
- Leaders Come From All Genders
- To Lead Sometimes the Best Thing to Do Is Serve
- A Good Leader Needs the Right Team

So there you have it! Thank you for coming along with us on this journey of leadership through the MCU and related films. In talking about leadership in these films, we connected those examples with research-supported relevant concepts that can be applied in your own leadership experiences. This book emphasized that we all engage in leadership and we all can improve at it.

We hope that you feel you learned something from this book and enjoyed yourself along the way. As you read this book, I'm sure you thought of other leadership examples in the Marvel films. There are many such examples to learn from in the films, but for book space purposes, we could only cover a few. There are also many other aspects of leadership theory and research that can be learned and applied to Marvel films. For now, those unfortunately will go unexamined (but most good superhero movies end up with sequels!). We do also encourage you to consider reading others books in the Exploring Effective Leadership Practices through Popular Culture series, as other volumes can help your learning of research-based leadership concepts, with many unique and not covered in this volume. They really are great reads!

So go out into the world and be the superhero leader your own organization needs!

# Appendix 1: Chapter Major Topics and Connected Films

| Title | Main Topics | Main Films |
|---|---|---|
| Chapter 1: How We See Leadership in the Marvel Cinematic Universe and How We See Leadership in General | I-O Psychology<br>Leadership as Process<br>Shared Leadership | N/A |
| Chapter 2: Who Has a Right to be the Leader? Leadership Transitions in Black Panther | Bases of Power<br>Leadership Transitions<br>Legitimacy | *Black Panther; Thor* |
| Chapter 3: Who Leads This Motley Crew? Shared and Team Leadership in the Guardians of the Galaxy | Shared Leadership<br>Team Leadership<br>Teams | *Guardians of the Galaxy; Guardians of the Galaxy Vol. 2* |
| Chapter 4: With Great Power Comes Great Responsibility: Mentorship and Spider-Man | Mentorship<br>Shared Vision | *Spider-Man: Into the Spider-Verse; Spider-Man; Spider-Man 2* |
| Chapter 5: How Do Leaders (Superheroes or Not) Deal With Conflict? | Conflict<br>Conflict Management<br>Creativity | *Avengers: Age of Ultron; Captain America: Civil War* |
| Chapter 6: Leadership During Crisis and Stress: Leadership During Stressful Times Like Thanos' "One Snap" | Crisis Leadership<br>Stress<br>Stress management | *The Avengers: Endgame; The Incredible Hulk* |
| Chapter 7: I Am Iron Man: Leader Authenticity, Self-awareness and Growth in Marvel Films | Authenticity<br>Authentic Leadership<br>Self-awareness | *The Avengers: Endgame; Iron Man; Iron Man 3* |
| Chapter 8: Should We Open Up Wakanda? Leader Roles in External Relations | External Environment<br>External Relationships<br>Teams | *Black Panther* |
| Chapter 9: Am I a Hero, an X-man, a Mutant, or Just a Menace? Leadership and Identity | Organizational Commitment<br>Organizational Identification<br>Sensemaking | *X-men; X-2; X-men: The Last Stand; X-men: Days of Future Past* |

| Title | Main Topics | Main Films |
|-------|-------------|------------|
| Chapter 10: Everything Begins With a (Her)o | Female Leadership<br><br>Implicit Leadership Theories Glass Ceiling/Cliff | *Avengers: Endgame; Captain Marvel* |
| Chapter 11: I Can Do This All Day: Steve Rogers, Servant Leader | Servant Leadership | *Marvel's The Avengers; Captain America: The First Avenger* |
| Chapter 12: Avengers Assemble: Forming Your Team Like a Leader | Recruitment<br><br>Selection | *Marvel's The Avengers; Iron Man 2; X-men; X-2* |
| Chapter 13: How You, True Believer, Can Lead Like a Superhero: Some General Takeaways on Leadership | Practical Takeaways | N/A |

# References

Andrews, J., & Clark, R. (2011). *Peer mentoring works!* Birmingham: Aston University.

Ashforth, B. E. (2016). Exploring identity and identification in organizations: Time for some course corrections. *Journal of Leadership & Organizational Studies, 23*, 361–373.

Ashforth, B. E. (2020). Identity and identification during and after the pandemic: How might COVID-19 change the research questions we ask? *Journal of Management Studies, 57*(8), 1763–1766.

Aurthur, K. (2021, April). Kevin Feige on Chloé Zhao's 'Spectacular' approach to 'Eternals' and who the film's 'Lead' character is. *Variety*. Retrieved from https://variety.com/2021/film/news/kevin-feige-chloe-zhao-eternals-1234962496/

Bergman, J. Z., Rentsch, J. R., Small, E. E., Davenport, S. W., & Bergman, S. M. (2012). The shared leadership process in decision-making teams. *The Journal of Social Psychology, 152*(1), 17–42.

Black, S. (2013). *Iron Man 3*. New York, NY: Marvel Studios.

Blader, S. L., Patil, S., & Parker, D. J. (2017). Organizational identification and workplace behavior: More than meets the eye. *Research in Organizational Behavior, 37*, 19–34.

Borden, A., & Fleck, R. (2019). *Captain Marvel*. New York, NY: Marvel Studios.

Bozeman, B., & Feeney, M. K. (2008). Mentor matching: A "goodness of fit" model. *Administration & Society, 40*(5), 465–482.

Bradley-Cole, K. (2021). Friend or fiend? An interpretative phenomenological analysis of moral and relational orientation in authentic leadership. *Leadership, 17*(4), 401–420.

Branagh, K. (2011). *Thor*. New York, NY: Marvel Studios.

Brandebo, M. F. (2020). Destructive leadership in crisis management. *Leadership & Organization Development Journal, 41*(4), 567–580.

Brown, M. E., & Treviño, L. K. (2006). Ethical leadership: A review and future directions. *The Leadership Quarterly, 17*(6), 595–616.

Carapinha, R., Ortiz-Walters, R., McCracken, C. M., Hill, E. V., & Reede, J. Y. (2016). Variability in women faculty's preferences regarding mentor similarity: A multi-institution study in academic medicine. *Academic Medicine : Journal of the Association of American Medical Colleges, 91*(8), 1108–1118. https://doi.org/10.1097/ACM.0000000000001284

Carson, J. B., Tesluk, P. E., & Marrone, J. A. (2007). Shared leadership in teams: An investigation of antecedent conditions and performance. *Academy of Management Journal, 50*(5), 1217–1234.

Carter, D. R., Cullen-Lester, K. L., Jones, J. M., Gerbasi, A., Chrobot-Mason, D., & Nae, E. Y. (2020). Functional leadership in interteam contexts: Understanding 'what' in the context of why? where? when? and who? *The Leadership Quarterly, 31*(1), 101378.

Cohen, S. (1980). After effects of stress on human performance and social behavior: A review of research and theory. *Psychological Bulletin, 88*, 82–108.

Conte, J. M., & Landy, F. J. (2019). *Work in the 21st century: An introduction to industrial and organizational psychology* (6th ed.). New York, NY: Wiley.

Coogler, R. (2018). *Black Panther*. New York, NY: Marvel Studios.

Cornu, R. L. (2005). Peer mentoring: Engaging pre-service teachers in mentoring one another. *Mentoring & Tutoring: Partnership in Learning, 13*(3), 355–366.

Daniels, L. (1991). *Marvel: Five fabulous decades of the world's greatest comics*. New York, NY: Harry N Abrams Inc.

De Dreu, C. K. W., & Nijstad, B. A. (2008). Mental set and creative thought in social conflict: Threat rigidity versus motivated focus. *Journal of Personality and Social Psychology, 95*(3), 648–661.

De Dreu, C. K. W., & Weingart, L. R. (2003). Task versus relationship conflict, team performance, and team member satisfaction: A meta-analysis. *Journal of Applied Psychology, 88*(4), 741–749.

De Waal, A., & Sivro, M. (2012). The relation between servant leadership, organizational performance, and the high-performance organization framework. *Journal of Leadership & Organizational Studies, 19*(2), 173–190.

Eby, L. T., Allen, T. D., Evans, S. C., Ng, T., & DuBois, D. L. (2008). Does mentoring matter? A multidisciplinary meta-analysis comparing mentored and non-mentored individuals. *Journal of Vocational Behavior, 72*(2), 254–267.

Ensher, E. A., & Murphy, S. E. (1997). Effects of race, gender, perceived similarity, and contact on mentor relationships. *Journal of Vocational Behavior, 50*(3), 460–481.

Faiz, N. (2013). Impact of manager's reward power and coercive power on employee's job satisfaction: A comparative study of public and private sector. *International Journal of Management and Business Research, 3*(4), 383–392.

Farmer, B. A., Slater, J. W., & Wright, K. S. (1998). The role of communication in achieving shared vision under new organizational leadership. *Journal of Public Relations Research, 10*(4), 219–235.

Favreau, J. (2008). *Iron Man*. New York, NY: Marvel Studios.

Favreau, J. (2010). *Iron Man 2*. New York, NY: Marvel Studios.

Finseraas, H., Johnsen, A. A., Kotsadam, A., & Torsvik, G. (2016). Exposure to female colleagues breaks the glass ceiling: Evidence from a combined vignette and field experiment. *European Economic Review, 90*, 363–374.

French, J. R. P., & Raven, B. H. (1959). The bases of social power. In D. Cartwright (Ed.), *Studies in Social Power* (pp. 150–167). Ann Arbor, MI: Institute for Social Research.

Froelich, K., McKee, G., & Rathge, R. (2011). Succession planning in nonprofit organizations. *Nonprofit Management and Leadership, 22*(1), 3–20.

Fulmer, R. M., Stumpf, S. A., & Bleak, J. (2009). The strategic development of high potential leaders. *Strategy & Leadership, 37*(3), 17–22. https://doi.org/10.1108/10878570910954600

George, B., Sims, P., McLean, A. N., & Mayer, D. (2007). Discovering your authentic leadership. *Harvard Business Review, 85*(2), 129.

Ghosh, R., & Reio, T. G., Jr. (2013). Career benefits associated with mentoring for mentors: A meta-analysis. *Journal of Vocational Behavior, 83*(1), 106–116.

Gino, F., Sezer, O., & Huang, L. (2020). To be or not to be your authentic self? Catering to others' preferences hinders performance. *Organizational Behavior and Human Decision Processes, 158*, 83–100.

Gipson, A. N., Pfaff, D. L., Mendelsohn, D. B., Catenacci, L. T., & Burke, W. W. (2017). Women and leadership: Selection, development, leadership style, and performance. *The Journal of Applied Behavioral Science, 53*(1), 32–65.

Glass, C., & Cook, A. (2016). Leading at the top: Understanding women's challenges above the glass ceiling. *The Leadership Quarterly, 27*, 51–63.

Goodwin, R. D., Dodson, S. J., Chen, J. M., & Diekmann, K. A. (2020). Gender, sense of power, and desire to lead: Why women don't "lean in" to apply for leadership groups that are majority-male. *Psychology of Women Quarterly, 44*(4), 468–487.

Grant Thornton. (2021). *Women in business report 2021: A window of opportunity*. Retrieved from https://www.grantthornton.global/en/insights/women-in-business-2021/

Greenleaf, R. K. (1970). *The Servant as a Leader*. Indianapolis, IN: Greenleaf Center.

Greer, C. R., & Virick, M. (2008). Diverse succession planning: Lessons from the industry leaders. *Human Resource Management, 47*(2), 351–367.

Griffeth, R. W., Hom, P. W., & Gaertner, S. (2000). A meta-analysis of antecedents and correlates of employee turnover: Update, moderators tests, and research implications for the next millennium. *Journal of Management, 26*(3), 463–488.

Groves, K. S. (2007). Integrating leadership development and succession planning best practices. *The Journal of Management Development, 26*(3), 239–260.

Guillaume, O., Honeycutt, A., & Savage-Austin, A. R. (2013). The impact of servant leadership on job satisfaction. *Journal of Business and Economics, 4*(5), 444–448.

Gunn, J. (2014). *Guardians of the galaxy.* New York, NY: Marvel Studios.

Gunn, J. (2017). *Guardians of the galaxy* (Vol. 2). New York, NY: Marvel Studios.

Hargis, M., & Watt, J. D. (2010). Organizational perception management: A framework to overcome crisis events. *Organization Development Journal, 28*(1), 73–87.

Harms, P. D., Crede, M., Tynan, M., Leon, M., & Jeung, W. (2017). Leadership and stress: A meta-analytic review. *The Leadership Quarterly, 28*, 178–194.

Harter, S. (2002). Authenticity. In C. R. Snyder & S. J. Lopez (Eds.), *Handbook of positive psychology* (pp. 382–394). New York, NY: Oxford University Press.

Hausknecht, J. P., Day, D. V., & Thomas, S. C. (2004). Applicant reactions to selection procedures: An updated model and meta-analysis. *Personnel Psychology, 57*, 639–683.

Hinchcliffe, E. (2021). The female CEOs on this year's Fortune 500 just broke three all-time records. *Fortune.* Retrieved from https://fortune.com/2021/06/02/female-ceos-fortune-500-2021-women-ceo-list-roz-brewer-walgreens-karen-lynch-cvs-thasunda-brown-duckett-tiaa/

Hogan, R., Curphy, G. J., & Hogan, J. (1994). What we know about leadership: Effectiveness and personality. *The American Psychologist, 49*(6), 493–504. https://doi.org/10.1037/0003-066X.49.6.493

Holbeche, L. (1996). Peer mentoring: The challenges and opportunities. *Career Development International, 1*(7), 24–27. https://doi.org/10.1108/13620439610152115

Hobbs, E., & Spencer, S. (2002). *Perceived Change in Leadership Skills as a Result of the Wilderness Education Association Wilderness Stewardship Course.* Paper presented at the Wilderness Education Association 2002 National Conference, Bradford Woods, IN.

Hoyland, T., Psychogios, A., Epitropaki, O., Damiani, J., Mukhuty, S., & Priestnall, C. (2021). A two-nation investigation of leadership self-perceptions and motivation to lead in early adulthood: The moderating role of gender and socio-economic status. *Leadership & Organization Development Journal, 42*(2), 289–315.

Hu, N., Chen, Z., Gu, J., Huang, S., & Liu, H. (2017). Conflict and creativity in inter-organizational teams: The moderating role of shared leadership. *The International Journal of Conflict Management, 28*(1), 74–102. https://doi.org/10.1108/IJCMA-01-2016-0003

Huizing, R. L. (2012). Mentoring together: A literature review of group mentoring. *Mentoring & Tutoring: Partnership in Learning, 20*(1), 27–55.

Ilgen, D. R., Major, D. A., Hollenbeck, J. R., & Sego, D. J. (1993). Team research in the 1990s. In M. M. Chemers & R. Ayman (Eds.), *Leadership theory and research: Perspectives and directions* (pp. 245–270). Cambridge, MA: Academic Press.

Jackson, D., Engstrom, E., & Emmers-Sommer, T. (2007). Think leader, think male *and* female: Sex vs. seating arrangement as leadership cues. *Sex Roles, 57*, 713–723.

Katz, D., & Kahn, R. L. (1978). *The social psychology of organizations.* New York, NY: Wiley.

Kaul, K. (2021). Refining the referral process: Increasing diversity for technology startups through targeted recruitment, screening and interview strategies. *Strategic HR Review, 20*(4), 125–129.

Kim, S. (2007). Learning goal orientation, formal mentoring, and leadership competence in HRD: A conceptual model. *Journal of European Industrial Training, 31*(3), 181–194.

Kim, J., Hsu, N., Newman, D. A., Harms, P. D., & Wood, D. (2020). Leadership perceptions, gender, and dominant personality: The role of normality evaluations. *Journal of Research in Personality, 87*, 1–9.

Koenig, A. M., Eagly, A. H., Mitchell, A. A., & Ristikari, T. (2011). Are leader stereotypes masculine? A meta-analysis of three research paradigms. *Psychological Bulletin, 137*(4), 616–642. https://doi.org/10.1037/a0023557

Kram, K. E. (1985). *Mentoring network: Developmental relationships in organisational life.* Glenview, IL: Scott Foreman.

Kristof, A. L. (1996). Person-organization fit: An integrative review of its conceptualizations, measurement, and implications. *Personnel Psychology, 49*, 1–49.

Lacerda, T. C. (2019). Crisis leadership in economic recession: A three-barrier approach to offset external constraints. *Business Horizons, 62*, 185–197.

Lee, E. K., Avgar, A. C., Park, W. W., & Choi, D. (2019). The dual effects of task conflict on team creativity: Focusing on the role of team-focused transformational leadership. *International Journal of Conflict Management, 30*(1), 132–154.

Lehman, D. W., O'Connor, K., Kovacs, B., & Newman, G. E. (2019). Authenticity. *Academy of Management Annals, 13*(1), 1–42.

Leterrier, L. (2008). *The Incredible Hulk.* New York, NY: Marvel Studios/Valhalla Motion Pictures.

Liden, R. C., Wayne, S. J., Liao, C., & Meuser, J. D. (2014). Servant leadership and serving culture: Influence on individual and unit performance. *Academy of Management Journal, 57*(5), 1434–1452.

Maitlis, S., & Christianson, M. (2014). Sensemaking in organizations: Taking stock and moving forward. *The Academy of Management Annals, 8*(1), 57–125.

McEntire, L. E., & Greene-Shortridge, T. M. (2011). Recruiting and selecting leaders for innovation: How to find the right leader. *Advances in Developing Human Resources, 13*(3), 266–278.

McFarland, L. A., & Ployhart, R. E. (2015). Social media: A contextual framework to guide research and practice. *Journal of Applied Psychology, 100*(6), 1653–1677. https://doi.org/10.1037/a0039244

Meyer, J. P., & Allen, N. J. (1991). A three-component conceptualization of organizational commitment. *Human Resource Management Review, 1*(1), 61–89.

Mikkelsen, E. N., & Wahlin, R. (2020). Dominant, hidden and forbidden sensemaking: The politics of ideology and emotions in diversity management. *Organization, 27*(4), 557–577.

Milosevic, I., Maric, S., & Lončar, D. (2020). Defeating the Toxic Boss: the nature of Toxic Leadership and the role of followers. *Journal of Leadership & Organizational Studies, 27*(2), 117–137.

Mitchell, M. E., Eby, L. T., & Ragins, B. R. (2015). My mentor, myself: Antecedents and outcomes of perceived similarity in mentoring relationships. *Journal of Vocational Behavior, 89*, 1–9. https://doi.org/10.1016/j.jvb.2015.04.008

Mumford, M. D., Zaccaro, S. J., Harding, F. D., Jacobs, T. O., & Fleishman, E. A. (2000). Leadership skills for a changing world: Solving complex social problems. *The Leadership Quarterly, 11*(1), 11–35.

Northouse, P. G. (2021). *Leadership: Theory and practice.* Sage publications

Oakes, P. (Director). (2020). The Marvel method (Season 1, Episode 7) [TV series episode]. In *Marvel 616.* Supper Club; Marvel Entertainment; Marvel New Media.

O'Brien, K. E., Biga, A., Kessler, S. R., & Allen, T. D. (2010). A meta-analytic investigation of gender differences in mentoring. *Journal of Management, 36*(2), 537–554. https://doi.org/10.1177/0149206308318619

Park, T. Y., & Shaw, J. D. (2013). Turnover rates and organizational performance: A meta-analysis. *Journal of Applied Psychology, 90*(2), 268–309.

Pearce, C. L., & Conger, J. A. (2003). *Shared leadership: Reframing the hows and whys of leadership.* London: Sage.

Persichetti, B., Ramsey, P., & Rothman, R. (2018). *Spider-Man: Into the spider-verse.* Los Angeles, CA: Columbia Pictures/Marvel Entertainment/Sony Pictures Animation.

Raimi, S. (2002). *Spider-man*. Los Angeles, CA: Columbia Pictures/Marvel Enterprises/ Laura Ziskin Production.

Raimi, S. (2004). *Spider-man 2*. Los Angeles, CA: Columbia Pictures/Marvel Enterprises/ Laura Ziskin Production.

Randall, K. R., Resick, C. J., & DeChurch, L. A. (2011). Building team adaptive capacity: The roles of sensegiving and team composition. *Journal of Applied Psychology, 96*(3), 525–540. https://doi.org/10.1037/a0022622

Rattner, B. (2006). *X-Men: The last stand*. Los Angeles, CA: Dune Entertainment/Marvel Entertainment/The Donners' Company/Ingenious Film Partner.

Reece, B. L., & Brandt, R. (1993). *Effective human relations in organisations* (5th ed.). Boston, MA: Houghton Mifflin.

Roth, K. (1995). Managing international interdependence: CEO characteristics in a resource-based framework. *Academy of Management Journal, 38*(1), 200–231.

Russo, A., & Russo, J. (2014). *Captain America: The winter soldier*. New York, NY: Marvel Studios.

Russo, A., & Russo, J. (2016). *Captain America: Civil war*. New York, NY: Marvel Studios.

Russo, A., & Russo, J. (2018). *Avengers: Infinity war*. New York, NY: Marvel Studios.

Russo, A., & Russo, J. (2019). *Avengers: Endgame*. New York, NY: Marvel Studios.

Scarlet, J., & Busch, J. (2016). Trauma shapes a hero. In T. Langley (Ed.), *Captain America vs. Iron Man: Freedom, security, psychology*. New York, NY: Sterling.

Schmidt, F. L., & Hunter, J. E. (1998). The validity of selection methods in personnel psychology: Practical and theoretical implications of 85 years of research findings. *Psychological Bulletin, 124*(2), 262–274.

Schneider, B., Goldstein, H. W., & Smith, D. B. (1995). The ASA framework: An update. *Personnel Psychology, 48*, 747–773.

Schriesheim, C. A. (1997). Substitutes-for-leadership theory: Development and basic concepts. *The Leadership Quarterly, 8*(2), 103–108. https://doi.org/10.1016/S1048-9843(97)90009-6

Scully, J. A., Tosi, H., & Banning. K. (2000). Life event checklists: Revisiting the social readjustment rating scale after 30 years. *Educational and Psychological Measurement, 60*, 864–876.

Shah, P. P., Peterson, R. S., Jones, S. L., & Ferguson, A. J. (2021). Things are not always what they seem: The origins and evolution of intragroup conflict. *Administrative Science Quarterly, 66*(2), 426–474.

Sheinfeld Gorin, S. N., Lee, R. E., & Knight, S. J. (2020). Group mentoring and leadership growth in behavioral medicine. *Translational Behavioral Medicine, 10*(4), 873–876.

Singer, B. (2000). *X-men*. Los Angeles, CA: Marvel Enterprises/The Donners' Company/ Bad Hat Harry Productions.

Singer, B. (2003). *X-2*. Los Angeles, CA: Marvel Enterprises/The Donners' Company/Bad Hat Harry Productions.

Singer, B. (2014). *X-men: Days of future past*. Los Angeles, CA: Marvel Entertainment/Bad Hat Harry/The Donners' Company/Genre Films/TSG Entertainment.

Smircich, L., & Morgan, G. (1982). Leadership: The management of meaning. *The Journal of Applied Behavioral Science, 18*(3), 257–273.

Sousa, M., & Van Dierendonck, D. (2016). Introducing a short measure of shared servant leadership impacting team performance through team behavioral integration. *Frontiers in Psychology, 6*, 2002.

Stead, V. (2005). Mentoring: A model for leadership development? *International Journal of Training and Development, 9*(3), 170–184. https://doi.org/10.1111/j.1468-2419.2005.00232.x

Van Dependence, D., & Nuijten, I. (2011). The servant leadership survey: Development and validation of a multidimensional measure. *Journal of Business and Psychology, 26*(3), 249–267.

van Esch, C., Luse, W., & Bonner, R. L. (2021). The impact of COVID-19 pandemic concerns and gender on mentor seeking behavior and self-efficacy. *Equality, Diversity and Inclusion: An International Journal*, Online First.

Volkema, R. J., & Bergmann, T. J. (1995). Conflict styles as indicators of behavioral patterns in interpersonal conflicts. *Journal of Social Psychology, 135*(1), 5–15.

Wageman, R., Hackman, J. R., & Lehman, E. (2005). Team diagnostic survey: Development of an instrument. *The Journal of Applied Behavioral Science, 41*(4), 373–398.

Walumbwa, F. O., Avolio, B. J., Gardner, W. L., Wernsing, T. S., & Peterson, S. J. (2008). Authentic leadership: Development and validation of a theory-based measure. *Journal of Management, 34*(1), 89–126.

Wetzel, S., & Wetzel, C. (2020). *The Marvel Studios story*. New York, NY: HarperCollins Leadership.

Whedon, J. (2012). *Marvel's The Avengers*. New York, NY: Marvel Studios.

Whedon, J. (2015). *Avengers: Age of Ultron*. New York, NY: Marvel Studios.

Whetten, D. A., & Cameron, K. S. (2020). *Developing management skills* (10th ed.). London: Pearson.

Whitten, S. (2021, January 31). The 13 highest-grossing film franchises at the box office. *CNBC*. Retrieved from https://www.cnbc.com/2021/01/31/the-13-highest-grossing-film-franchises-at-the-box-office.html

Yahaya, R., & Ebrahim, F. (2016). Leadership styles and organizational commitment: Literature review. *Journal of Management Development, 35*(2), 190–216.

Yukl, G. A., & Gardner, W. L. (2020). *Leadership in organizations* (9th ed.). London: Pearson.

Zaccaro, S. J., Rittman, A. L., & Marks, M. A. (2001). Team leadership. *The Leadership Quarterly, 12*(4), 451–483. https://doi.org/10.1016/S1048-9843(01)00093-5

# Index

In this volume of *Exploring Effective Leadership Practices through Popular Culture*, Schmidt and Islam examine how you can learn about research and evidence-based leadership concepts through examples drawn from the popular MCU movies and related superhero films.

*Leaders Assemble! Leadership in the MCU* includes sound research and evidence-based advice on how to improve as a leader on topics such as leadership development, conflict management, mentorship, sensemaking, shared leadership, servant leadership, authentic leadership, servant leadership, and selecting your team. Examples from your favorite MCU films make these concepts come alive so you can easily see how they can be used to improve your own leadership skills.

Each chapter focuses on a core leadership concept and shows you how you can use it to be a successful leader, with MCU films and superheroes leading the way with relevant examples, before finally summarizing the main points you can use in your own leadership practice.

**GORDON B. SCHMIDT**, PhD, is a Professor of Management at the University of Louisiana Monroe. He researches the Future of Work, leadership and/or motivation in varied contexts including lean production and Corporate Social Responsibility and consults with organizations on these topics.

**SY ISLAM** is a co-founder and Vice President of Consulting with Talent Metrics and an Associate Professor of Industrial Organizational psychology at Farmingdale State College. Dr. Islam won the Society for Industrial-Organizational Psychology's Scientist-Practitioner Presidential Recognition Award for his focus on science driven practices in training and talent development and the Farmingdale State College Center for Technology, Learning, and Teaching's Faculty Mentorship award.

LEADERS ASSEMBLE: LEADERSHIP IN THE M
SCHMIDT

9781801176736-8513-355971
111-6636266-3213809

**USED**

OR-18332-173158

MTSU / 2024 / FALL MGMT 3850 1

emera
PUBLISHIN